The Diary of Emily Caroline Creaghe, Explorer

The Diary of
Emily Caroline Creaghe

Explorer

Edited with an introduction by Peter Monteath

Wakefield
Press

Wakefield Press
16 Rose Street
Mile End
South Australia 5031
www.wakefieldpress.com.au

First published by Corkwood Press 2004
This Wakefield Press edition published 2021

Copyright enquiries concerning the diary should be directed to the
State Library of New South Wales

All rights reserved. This book is copyright. Apart from any
fair dealing for the purposes of private study, research,
criticism or review, as permitted under the Copyright Act,
no part may be reproduced without written permission.
Enquiries should be addressed to the publisher.

Original cover concept by Diana V. Smith and Michael Pomeroy Smith

ISBN 978 1 74305 666 0

 A catalogue record for this book is available from the National Library of Australia

 Wakefield Press thanks Coriole Vineyards for continued support

Contents

Foreword to the 2021 edition — vii

Acknowledgements — ix

A Note on the Text — xi

Introduction — 1

The Diary of Emily Caroline Creaghe, Explorer — 15

Appendix

    Poems — 101

    Recipes — 103

    Letter to Creaghe's Father, Major George Cayley Robinson — 106

Afterword — 109

Index — 115

Foreword to the 2021 Edition

Much has happened since the diary of Emily Caroline Creaghe was published in 2004, transforming a little known artefact of Australia's colonial past into a text accessible to all. It was launched by Valmai Hankel, herself an intrepid traveller, whose knowledge of the Australian outback is matched by few. Then one of its readers, the artist Gemma Lynch-Memory, was inspired to retrace the steps of Emily Caroline Creaghe across Queensland and the Northern Territory, and to produce a national touring exhibition under the title 'emily: explorer'. Some years later, Anna Banfi, an Italian editor and traveller who had her own memories of remote Australia, devoted herself to the diary's translation and the publication of an Italian edition. For these and countless other women, travel through places far from home has become almost commonplace – at least until COVID-19 intervened. Literally and metaphorically, they explore in the footsteps of the world's Emily Caroline Creaghes.

Since that time, too, interest among Australians in their history of vexed race relations has grown exponentially. This is especially evident in the attention paid to the dispossession of First Nations peoples, as the colonial frontier was pushed relentlessly from the initially tiny and precarious coastal settlements across a vast continent. As we understand more clearly today, this was not a matter of exploring and occupying a mythical *terra nullius*. Rather, it was a process stained with violence and bloodshed. Its origins commonly lay in exploratory expeditions like that undertaken by Emily Caroline Creaghe.

This new edition of Creaghe's diary is a timely reminder of the courage, tenacity and resilience of an extraordinary woman. More than that, it confronts us with the troubling realities of Australia's fast-moving nineteenth-century frontiers. It deserves to be read with unflinching attention, not just as a record of its own time and place, but as a traveller's guide to the Australia we seek to understand today.

Peter Monteath

E. Carrie Creaghe
The Little Explorer's Diary

Letts's
AUSTRALASIAN
DIARY
AND ALMANAC
FOR
1883

BEING THE FORTY-SIXTH YEAR OF THE REIGN OF HER
MAJESTY QUEEN VICTORIA—(*Accession June 20, 1837*).

OCTAVO EDITION.

PRINTED AND PUBLISHED FOR EXPORT IN JULY, 1882, BY

LETTS, SON & CO. LIMITED, LONDON.

[ENTERED AT STATIONERS' HALL.]

Acknowledgements

The explorer's diary of Caroline Creaghe was able to make the long trek from the ink-filled pages of *Letts's Australasian Diary and Almanac* for 1983 to this published edition only with the invaluable help of quite a number of individuals and institutions.

The Northern Territory Archives Service provided a Northern Territory History Grant in 2003 which enabled work to begin. Above all it made possible a transcription of the original diary, most of which was undertaken by Michael Foster, who did an excellent job with a very difficult manuscript, which in many parts bordered on the indecipherable. Michael also followed the trail of Caroline Creaghe into archives and libraries, and in doing so built the foundation for the editing of the diary and the provision of a critical introduction.

Jennifer Broomhead at the Mitchell Library in the State Library of New South Wales gave me access to the original diary, supplied information about its provenance, and helped locate relevant images to accompany the text. Both Valerie Sitters and Annette Mills at the State Library of South Australia provided invaluable leads in the search for material relating to Ernest Favenc and his 1883 expedition. Similarly, Tony Roberts was able to make some very timely and helpful suggestions. Having devoted vast efforts to the research for his forthcoming book *Frontier Justice: A History of the Gulf Country to 1900*, he helped me to understand better the historical context of the expedition and provided details which helped to put many pieces of the story into place.

The images which accompany the text were made available through Copying Services at the State Library of New South Wales and the State Library of South Australia. Both those libraries, the Battye Library in Perth and the Smith family in Sydney are thanked for granting permission to use images reproduced here. In addition, I thank Peter Donovan for permission to use his map of early explorations of the Northern Territory.

ACKNOWLEDGEMENTS

All the other maps are the work of Diana and her husband Michael Pomeroy Smith, whose architectural talents have been deployed here to great effect in the service of history. The striking cover design similarly attests to their creative talents. Thanks also go to the book's designer David Hayes, who, having been presented with a disparate collection of texts and images, was able to synthesise them into the book before you. Richard Barnes of Corkwood Press, Hyde Park Press in Adelaide, and Charlie Zamut of Chasdoor Binding all played their roles in making the final product as handsome as it is.

Finally, my sincere thanks go to Diana V. Smith, the granddaughter of the remarkable Caroline Creaghe, who in the end committed more hours to the preparation of a meticulous transcription using the original document and to carrying out invaluable research in the Mitchell Library than she might care to remember. Without her initial commitment to the project, and without her unstinting support, both moral and practical, in guiding things through to a successful conclusion, this book would not have come about.

A Note on the Text

Caroline Creaghe's Diary was written in the 1883 edition of *Letts's Australian Diary and Almanac*. Typically at the end of the day she would record her experiences and impressions, often in the most trying of circumstances. It would have been no easy matter, especially in a dying or faint light, to find ink and pen and to recall in writing, with remarkable few false starts and errors, the events of the day. Bearing those conditions in mind, as well as the physical and mental exhaustion of long-distance travel, the neatness and consistency of much of the script is striking, and presumably stems from many years of practice at school in England.

Nonetheless, being aware that the diary was both unique and fragile, and that the older style of writing was no longer easily decipherable, Caroline's youngest son, Evelyn Roy Barnett (Roy), made a transcription of it in his own neat handwriting some time in the last years of Caroline's life. He did so in direct collaboration with his mother. At this time Caroline crossed out some passages in the original diary, even perhaps using Roy's pen and ink, as the colour of the ink seems identical with his. Roy was later to tell his daugher that Caroline did not want to offend Mrs. Favenc or any others mentioned in the library who might still be alive. It was that daughter, and Caroline's youngest grand-daughter, Diana V. Smith, who in 1977, under her father's guidance, prepared a faithful, typewritten version of her father's transcription. It is deposited in the Mitchell Library with the original diary, with two maps prepared by her and her husband Michael Pomeroy Smith, and with transcriptions of a small number of newspaper items relating to the Creaghes and the 1883 expedition.

The two versions of the transcription include some additions which were made to the original diary, in most cases in pencil. It is not known when these additions to the diary were made. It is possible that in the dark, or after packing away for the night, pencil was Caroline's only option; it might also be that the additions in pencil were made at a later point to supplement the original record. This cannot be determined with any certainty. In any case, it is evident that Caroline herself was responsible for them, so they have been included as part of the text here in the interest of reproducing the text of the diary itself with all possible accuracy. However, footnotes indicate which parts of the text were added and in what form.

In some minor respects the transcriptions vary from the original, but for the purposes of this publication every effort has been made to follow the diary, not the transcriptions, useful though the latter certainly were in deciphering some difficult parts of the original. Most notably the transcriptions make a small number of omissions. This applies above all to the final stages of the expedition in Darwin and the return voyage. These may simply have been regarded as less important or less interesting than the exploratory expedition proper, though in reality they provide fascinating insights into life into the colonial history of both the Northern Territory and North Queensland. In any case, those earlier omissions from the diary have been restored in this version of the text.

The transcriptions also omit a number of undated writings found in the back of the diary. Some of these – a couple of poems, presumably, but not verifiably, the work of Caroline, and a number of recipes – have been reproduced here in an appendix to the diary. The recipes clearly relate back to the expedition, since they include such standard explorer fare as damper, but also a number of recipes obtained from Carl Creek, including Numinum Cake and Guava Jelly! Other elements, among them quite detailed cash accounts and some knitting patterns, have been omitted, since they appear to stem from a later period when Caroline had a newborn child. A couple of formulae for remedies – one for dysentery and one for neuralgia, which indeed afflicted Harry during the expedition – are also among the jottings in the back of the diary, but they are not reproduced here. However, a letter to Caroline's father, Major George Cayley Robinson, has been included, since it stems from the expedition. Dated 12 July 1883, it was written when Caroline was at the Katherine Telegraph Station. Alas, it is incomplete, but it offers insights into the state of the expedition at that point as well as the nature of her relationship with her father.

The diary initially follows the diary's headings (1 Monday, 2 Tuesday and so on), but eventually some very lengthy entries, which required more space than the diary allowed, forced Caroline from mid-April to cross out the diary's dates and provide her own (16th Monday, 17th Tuesday etc.) This change has been followed here, and, as in the original diary, the relevant month is recorded at the top of each page.

To convey to the reader a clear sense of place, Diana and Michael Pomeroy Smith have kindly prepared a series of meticulously drawn maps, which, on the basis of the information provided in the diary, indicate as truly as possible just where Caroline and her fellow-expeditioners were during their many months on the move. In their entirety, they also convey some idea of the scale of the achievement involved in trekking from Normanton to Darwin.

Finally, and in the hope of complementing the often striking images delivered by Caroline's written word, a number of images have been added. They were not part of the original diary – which was quite devoid of illustration – but they introduce us to some of the characters encountered along the way, and, taken together with the words of an accomplished diarist, they help to bring back to life the interesting times of Caroline Creaghe.

Emily Caroline Creaghe

INTRODUCTION

Caroline Creaghe was a born traveller. Her mother, Mary Harriet Robinson (b.1830), gave birth to her on the 1st of November 1860 while sailing on a British ship through the Bay of Bengal. Her parents named her Emily Caroline Robinson, though later she was to omit the "Emily" and preferred to call herself simply "Carrie". Her father, Major George Cayley Robinson (b. 1824), an officer in the Royal Artillery, had just spent a period of leave in England and was returning to service in India when his daughter was born. The family's connections with India were very strong – Mary was the daughter of a Major Woodward, who also served in the British Army in India.

Some of Caroline's early life was thus spent in India. But in late 1865, and after some twenty years of service, health problems persuaded her father to retire from the army. The family moved to England, where Caroline received her formal education at a school in Weston Super Mare near Bristol. In 1876, and with Caroline still in her mid-teens, the family chose to migrate to Australia. After their arrival in Sydney they boarded for a time in Wynyard Square before taking up residence in Lavender Bay. They were known to worship regularly at St. Thomas's Church in North Sydney.

It was not in Sydney but in Queensland, to be more precise in Goodna just outside Brisbane, and during a visit to her sister and brother-in-law that Caroline met her future husband, Harry Alington Creaghe. Harry hailed from an aristocratic Irish background; indeed, he could boast the Marquess of Ormonde as his grandfather. In 1865, and at the age of just 16, he had come to Australia aboard the *Young Australia*. Since then he had gathered a good deal of experience working in rural Queensland. At first he was employed at Cleveland near Brisbane by Captain Hope, formerly of the Coldstream Guards and a brother of the then Earl of Hopetoun. After about a year he moved north, still in the service of Captain Hope, to the Comet Creek area in Central Queensland. The property where he now worked, "Albinia Downs", ran mainly sheep and extended over a huge area. The isolation and loneliness of acting as an overseer at an outstation far from the head station caused him to be homesick for his native Ireland; it may also account for a breakdown he suffered there, and for which he was treated at a Mental Home in Goodna, just to the west of Brisbane. Although it was misfortune which had brought him to Goodna, the outcome was a happy one, since it was there that he met his wife-to-be. Caroline's brother-in-law, Dr Lamb, was the medical superindendent in Goodna, and during Harry's convalescence Caroline visited her sister and Dr Lamb at the Home. When Harry and Caroline married in the last month of 1881 he was 32 years of age to her 21. They soon produced their first child, Cayley, who however died very young, apparently from drinking contaminated water.[1] It was a devastating experience for both parents; thereafter Caroline resolved never to travel with a baby again and, as we shall see, returned to Sydney after her northern expedition for the birth of her second child.

Perhaps a need to put that personal tragedy behind them persuaded Caroline and Harry to try something quite new. Or perhaps the possibility of founding a new life in the tropical north of Australia, where work was available for a man of Harry's skills and experience, seemed attractive at that time. Whatever the motivation, they elected to participate in an exploratory party which, if successful, would take them through some harsh and challenging terrain, from Normanton in North Queensland to Port Darwin in what was then South Australia's Northern Territory. We do not know the exact circumstances in which this daunting and yet tantalizing prospect presented itself, but we do know that the man who presented it to them was Ernest Favenc.

Exploring the North

He may not have a prominent place in the annals of Australian exploration, but Ernest Favenc did much to fill in some of the gaps in the maps of Australia's outback. Born in England, he was educated at Temple College in Cowley, Oxfordshire, as well as at the Werderscher

---

1 To compound the tragedy, records suggest that another son, Robert, also died in the same year. If a twin of Cayley, as seems probable, Robert might have been stillborn.

Gymnasium in Berlin. In 1863, at just eighteen years of age, Favenc moved to Australia, initially to Sydney, and then after a year to North Queensland.

At that time the general shape of the northern coast was well enough known, thanks in no small part to the hydrographic work of Matthew Flinders aboard the *Investigator* in 1802. But European knowledge of the northern interior, even after the explorations of such people as Ludwig Leichhardt and Edmund Kennedy, remained at best patchy. The German Leichhardt led an expedition from the Darling Downs in October of 1844 with Port Essington, a small outpost on the Cobourg Peninsula, his goal. He famously lost his companion John Gilbert in a fatal altercation with Aborigines in June of the following year, but with the remaining seven members of his party he finally reached his destination at the end of 1845.

A decade later a further expedition was organized to explore Australia's far north, but this time from west to east. Led by Augustus Gregory, the party sailed first to the estuary of the Victoria River, which it explored before pushing east to the Elsey, Roper and McArthur Rivers and eventually, after some sixteen months, back to Brisbane.

Further important breakthroughs in establishing the general contours of the interior of the Northern Territory came with the 1861–62 expedition led by John McDouall Stuart. After one failed attempt he managed to do what Burke and Wills so tragically had not, that is, he completed his trek to the continent's north coast and made it back to the south as well. Moreover, he returned with an extraordinarily sanguine assessment of the North's potential for development: "If this country is settled, it will be one of the finest colonies under the Crown, suitable for the growth of any and everything – what a splendid country for producing cotton!"[2] Stuart's optimism was infectious. It spread not only to his paymasters in the South Australian Government but also to capitalist interests in the colony.

---

2   John McDouall Stuart, *J. McDouall Stuart's Explorations across the Continent of Australia, 1861–1862*, Melbourne: 1863, p. 57.

In the hope that the putative wealth of the North would fall into South Australian hands the government campaigned for the annexation of the Northern Territory. In doing so South Australia had to compete with the claims of its rival colony, Queensland. The argument was won in the favour of South Australia in 1863, thanks in no small part to Stuart's heroic efforts, sponsored as they had been by the South Australian government. Thereafter it supported further exploration and surveying of the north, some of it performed by John McKinlay, who in 1865 ventured north to the Alligator River. It was there that he was trapped by flood waters, but in a demonstration of admirable ingenuity under pressure – he constructed a raft from his horses' hides – McKinlay staged his own rescue and made his way to the coast and safety.

It was the South Australian government too which threw its support behind the construction of an Overland Telegraph Line which, it was reasoned, would play an important role in bringing the southern colony and its northern extension together. The construction of the line was preceded by an exploratory party, which was led by John Ross, and which established an appropriate route. Nonetheless, the project of constructing the line took longer and was more expensive than at first thought. Not until 22 August 1872, and at a place called Ironstone Ponds, was it completed. Two wires from opposing directions were connected; Port Augusta was connected with Port Darwin, and Australia thereby with the rest of the world. Along the line were numerous stations, some of which, as we shall see, came to be greeted by travellers and explorers such as Caroline Creaghe and Ernest Favenc as life-saving havens.

This is not to say that Queenslanders lost interest in the Northern Territory. If the hope of annexation had to be abandoned, the Territory still beckoned as a kind of western frontier, especially after pastoral and mining interests pushed westward across large tracts of north Queensland in the 1860s. Among those whose gaze shifted to the still largely unknown West was Gresley Lukin, the proprietor of the *Brisbane Courier* and of the *Queenslander*, who put up money to support an expedition from Queensland to Port Darwin, following a line which, as the longer-term plans had it, might be followed by a railway. The man Lukin chose to lead the

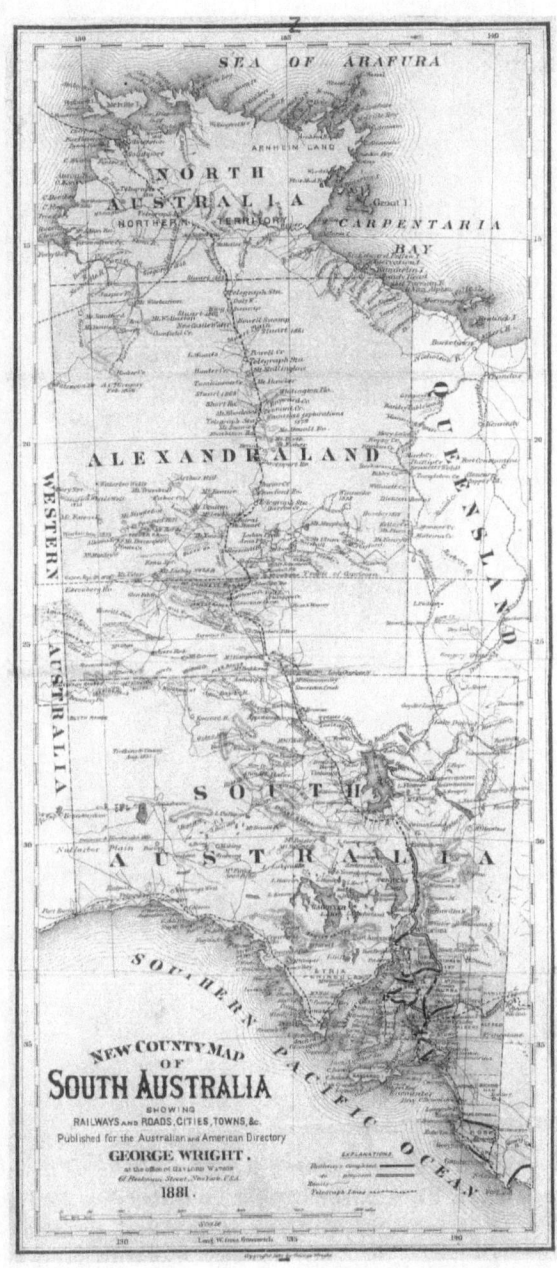

Map of South Australia 1881 by George Wright
State Library of New South Wales

Portrait of Ludwig Leichhardt, drawn by Isobel Fox 28 May 1846
State Library of New South Wales

expedition was none other than Favenc, who had garnered wide experience of the north, and whose brief was now to plot the general course of the proposed line, to explore the country through which it would run, and to assess its suitability for pastoral and mining activity.

Alas, despite the efforts of Favenc and Lukin, the railway line never eventuated, though the expedition cannot be written off as a failure. Setting off from Blackall on 19 July 1878, Favenc and his companions headed north-west to reach the Burke River and then the Herbert (now the Georgina), which they followed north. Even then they had not yet managed to exceed the reach of European civilization, since they came across travelling cattle. The party explored a number of creeks in the region, including Birthday Creek, named by Favenc to commemorate his birthday on the day of discovery, but its members were unimpressed with the desolate landscape. By December the expedition was beginning to suffer from a combination of heat and shortage of fresh water; the horses in particular were tormented by thirst. Indeed it was the dryness of the landscape which for a time prevented Favenc from pushing west to the Telegraph Line. From there they they would be able to proceed northward to complete the journey to Port Darwin and its settlement at Palmerston. Not until January of 1879 did Favenc make a final push for the Line, from which he could telegraph news of the party's arrival and survival to Brisbane, where no doubt it was received with some relief. In mid-March Favenc and his companions reached Palmerston, from where they returned to Brisbane by boat.

Though aware of the hardship suffered by Favenc and his companions, Lukin's own assessment was resolutely up-beat. "With the exception of isolated and comparatively small patches, the whole interior is capable of being immediately transformed into one vast sheep and cattle run, and in due course much of it will no doubt be fit for agriculture. The country is there; it is for us go to and take possession of it."[3]

---

3   Editorial, *Queenslander*, 18 January 1879. Cited in Cheryl Frost, *The Last Explorer: The Life and Work of Ernest Favenc*, Townsville: Foundation for Australian Literary Studies, 1983, p. 25.

In November of the following year, 1880, Favenc's life took a new turn – he married Bessie Matthews, whom he had known for some years. Married life though did not put an end to his explorations, and his focus remained firmly on the Northern Territory, where hopes for the pastoral industry were still high. In 1882 he explored the area between Creswell Creek and the Telegraph Line and attempted – unsuccessfully – to reach the Gulf of Carpentaria along the rivers to the east of Creswell Creek.[4]

THE 1883 EXPEDITION

Acutely aware of the financial commitment it had made to the Territory in the form of the Telegraph Line, and conscious of continuing Queensland designs on its western frontier, the South Australian government had a vested interest in the commercial exploitation of its Northern Territory. Attempts had been made, both in England and in South Australia, to sell blocks of land in the Territory, but with limited success. The discovery of gold in the early 1870s had brought a renewed burst of optimism, only to prove ill-founded. In time European interests abandoned the Territory gold fields, which gave up their wealth so meanly; it was above all the Chinese who persevered. By the 1880s the main hope lay with the cattle industry. In particular the region between the Telegraph Line to the west and the already stocked stations of Queensland to the east held promise, but it was territory with which Europeans were not well acquainted. Even if the land were ideal for grazing, the question presented itself as to how produce might be transported to centres of population. With its miniscule European population, the Northern Territory by itself was a market with bleak prospects.

At this crucial time of both private and state interest in the commercial development of the far north, Favenc offered his services as an already accomplished explorer with direct and recent experience of the territory in question. He was later to present a report to the South Australian Parliament on his findings, which indicates

---

4   H.J. Gibbney, "Ernest Favenc", in *Australian Dictionary of Biography, vol. 4: 1851–1890*, Melbourne: MUP, 1972, p. 160.

that he had government interests in mind.⁵ But it is also clear that he was acting at least in part on behalf of private pastoral interests, which would have been keen to receive a candid assessment of the region's potential as grazing land.⁶ Favenc's plan was to proceed west from Queensland, traverse territory which was still in large part *terra incognita*, assess the suitability of the land for stocking, and explore the possibility of using the river system – and in particular the McArthur River – to transport produce.

Favenc arranged to take his young wife, Bessie, with him. Exactly why Favenc also invited Harry and Caroline Creaghe to join the expedition is unclear. Harry Creaghe, like Favenc himself, could already boast extensive cattle station experience in Queensland, and that might well have appeared attractive to Favenc. From Harry's viewpoint, perhaps there was the hope that the expedition might reveal some new land which he might settle. As for Caroline, Favenc might well have thought of her as an appropriate companion for Bessie, who presumably would not have welcomed the prospect of being the expedition's sole female member.

---

5   On 21 February 1883 Favenc wrote from Sydney to the South Australia minister responsible for the Northern Territory, John Langdon Parson, with the following offer: "Sir, I am about starting to explore the district south of the Gulf of Carpentaria watered by the Macarthur, Robertson and Calvert Rivres. As it is of some interest to determine the description of country between the upper tablelands and the coast, I will be glad to furnish your government an accurate report of the country pass over. In return I would ask for an official recognition of the expedition, and the Government of S Australia may depend upon my using the best endeavours to maintain peacable relations with the Native tribes. I have the honour to be Yours Obediently, Ernest Favenc." State Records of South Australia GRS 1/1883/706.

6   Favenc himself in 1908 wrote that in 1883 he had been "on a private expedition to report on pastoral country". In particular, as Tony Roberts has established, Favenc was hired by Andrew Broad, a partner of Alexander and Robert Amos, to explore some of the huge amounts of land they had taken up in the Northern Territory. They all lived in Sydney, but their station, McArthur River, comprised more than 47 000 square kilometres of the distant Northern Territory. See Ernest Favenc, *The Explorers of Australia and Their Life-Work*, Christchurch: Whitcombe & Tombs Ltd., 1908, p. 227, and Tony Roberts, *Frontier Justice: A History of the Gulf Country to 1900*, St. Lucia: Queensland University Press, 2005, chapter 8.

A curious choice though it may seem, given the well established facts about the dangers and hardships inevitably to be faced, it is conceivable that the presence of women in the party was condoned, if not even suggested, by the South Australian government. There was, it seems, a precedent dating from very early in the colony's history. A certain Eliza Davies, a native of Scotland, took part in an exploratory expedition headed by Charles Sturt and covering the region between the northwest bend of the Murray River and the Gulf of St. Vincent. Accompanying her were, among others, Governor Gawler's daughter Julia and Mrs. Sturt. In her memoirs Eliza Davies recalls: "I heard a conversation between high officals, from which I learned that the policy of taking ladies with them, and bringing all back in safety, would ensure a readier sale of land in England. Capitalists would not fear the savages when ladies had traversed the country in safety."[7] Just as the sale of land was crucial to the financial well-being of the colony in its early years, so was the sale of its Northern Territory land in the 1880s.

The final member of the expedition was to be Lindsay Crawford, a native of Adelaide, where he was born in 1852. Indeed, Crawford could boast intimate connections with Adelaide's early Establishment, since he was the son of E. J. F. Crawford, who headed a respectable brewing family. Moreover, his mother was a sister of George Fife Angas's partner Charles Flaxman. Despite his promising pedigree Crawford's career was chequered. He trained as a telegraph operator, then turned his hand to brewing, visited New Zealand to expand his knowledge of the business, but then made his way to the Northern Territory to start his own business there. Failure persuaded him to try gold mining, also in the Northern Territory, but the demise of that venture soon drove him back to telegraphy. From 1874 to 1877 he was employed by the South Australian Telegraph Service at Powell's Creek on the still relatively new Telegraph Line. Thereafter he moved to Southport, on the southern arm of Port Darwin, where for a few months he ran a store which followed a trajectory similar to his previous enterprises. He

---

7   Eliza Davies, *The Story an of Earnest Life: A Woman's Adventures in Australia, and in Two Voyages Around the World*, Cincinnati: Central Book Concern, 1881, p. 121.

returned to telegraphy, but clearly was open to other possibilities when Favenc approached him to participate in the expedition. Crawford offered years of invaluable experience in the Northern Territory, as well as a youthful hope that he might yet make his future and his fortune in the north.

THE JOURNEY BEGINS

Caroline Creaghe's diary entries begin on the first day of the year 1883, when she and her husband Harry arrived in Bowen. The diary then follows the remainder of the voyage to Townsville, Port Douglas, Cooktown and then on to Thursday Island, where they joined Favenc and his wife Bessie. From there the journey proceeded on board the *Truganini*, which delivered them to Normanton on 17 January.

Had Bessie Favenc enjoyed more robust health at the time, she would have shared with Caroline Creaghe the honour of being the first woman to participate in a formal exploring party in northern Australia. As it happened, she reported in Normanton that she was not well enough to travel overland. It was decided that she would return to Sydney with her husband; Caroline and Harry would simply have to await Favenc's return.[8] They did so, as the reader will find, for the most part at Lilydale station on Carl Creek south-west of Burketown, owned by Francis Shadforth.

From the time of Bessie's unscheduled departure, Caroline was alone among male company. The unaccustomed challenges of enduring a northern summer soon relegated to the background any concerns she might have harboured about her predicament as a lone woman among men. That her constitution was at least as well equipped as that of the men to deal with the perils of heat, exhaustion and disease was soon to be proved in tragic circumstances. One of the men accompanying her on the party headed inland, Warner, was afflicted by sunstroke and died, as Caroline records, in great agony.

---

8 According to Cheryl Taylor, the Favencs' second child (the first, Amy Eleanor, was born in September 1881) was stillborn "probably in early 1883". In all likelihood then it was pregnancy which prohibited Bessie's participation and forced her return to Sydney. See Cheryl Taylor, "Introduction", in Taylor (ed.), *Ernest Favenc. Tales of the Austral Tropics*, Sydney: UNSW Press, 1997, p. xvii.

The enforced delay at Carl Creek was trying enough. For a time a bout of sandy blight, which left her "blind in one eye and nearly so in the other", interrupted the keeping of a diary. The news brought by Harry some two-and-a-half months later – on 11 April – that Favenc had returned from Sydney must have brought great relief. Even more welcome, for Caroline at least, was the additional announcement that she would indeed be permitted to join the expedition proper, which could now at long last begin. Her response, as she records it, was one of "intense delight".

The Creaghes rejoined Favenc at Gregory Downs station a couple of days later. It was there also that they met Lindsay Crawford for the first time. On the following day, 14 April 1883, the expedition to the still largely unknown territory to the west could commence.

As was the case on Favenc's *Queenslander* expedition, the broad aim was to proceed to the Telegraph Line and then, having joined it, to follow it to Port Darwin. Creaghe's diary records the variety of landscapes they traversed on the way there. Much of it appeared hostile and unwelcoming to a European gaze, but on the 23rd of April they camped beside a large and beautiful lagoon which Favenc was to name the "Caroline". Eventually the party reached the Telegraph Line and the station at Powell's Creek, where at last Caroline was to find much needed rest.

FAVENC'S MCARTHUR RIVER EXPEDITION

It was at this point that the party temporarily separated. There are signs in Creaghe's diary that by that time the separation was welcome. The condition both of horses and humans was such that the planned exploration of the McArthur River by the entire party was out of the question. Favenc, Crawford, a recent acquaintance by the name of Rogers, and the healthiest of the horses thus departed to the east in search of the McArthur, while Caroline and Harry rested before resuming their trek up the Telegraph Line.

The McArthur River leg of the expedition is of course not described in Creaghe's diary, but it was recorded by Favenc. He was to write an official account of the leg and furnish it with a detailed

Ernest Favenc. Photograph by L. W. Appleby, Sydney.
State Library of New South Wales

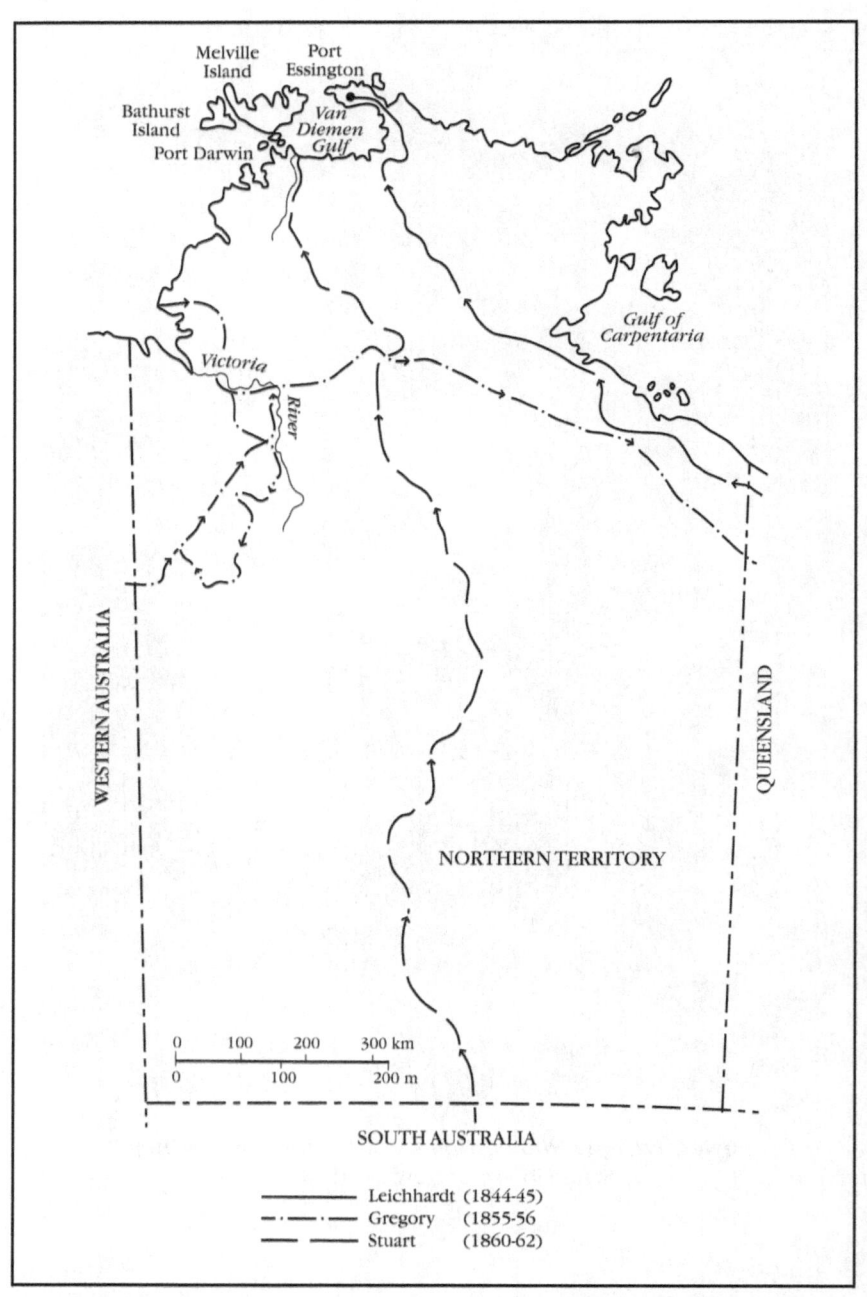

Routes of Northern Explorers 1844–62.
Courtesy Peter Donovan

map, both of which were presented to the South Australian government and published in the *Proceedings of the Parliament of South Australia* in 1883–84.[9] Another version of events was published for popular consumption in *The Sydney Mail*.[10] In some respects more interesting though is Favenc's handwritten diary of that expedition-within-an-expedition, the original of which is held in the Mitchell Library in Sydney. Just as Creaghe's diary suggests that she had grown weary of Favenc's company, his diary implies that the feeling was mutual. In the entry for the day of their departure from Powell's Creek, that is, 28 May 1883, Favenc records the presence of their new companion, Rogers. Of the latter he writes: "Rogers seems inclined to develop a conversational talent but is a handy man and will be useful. More so than our late companions who were only ornamental."[11]

As Favenc, Crawford and the loquacious Rogers made their way successfully to the McArthur, Caroline and Harry followed the Telegraph Line north, taking the weaker horses with them, and with Katherine Station as their destination. They arrived there on 14 June and awaited the arrival of Favenc and Crawford and the reuniting of the group. It was during this waiting period that Caroline and Harry were able to visit the nearby Springvale Station, managed by Alfred Giles and owned by Dr W.J. Browne. The Giles brothers had overlanded stock to Springvale for Browne, who was one of very few South Australians with pastoral interests in the Territory at the time.[12] That visit is recorded in the recollections of Alfred Giles, published in the *North Queensland Register* many years later under the title

---

9 "Reports on Country in the Northern Territory. Order by the House of Assembly to be printed and plan lithographed, October 9th, 1883", *Proceedings of the Parliament of South Australia 1883–4. Vol. IV.* Adelaide:Government Printer, 1884, No. 181.
10 Ernest Favenc, "Diary of a Trip from North Newcastle to Macarthur River" Part 1, *The Sydney Mail*, 24.11.1883, pp. 969–70; Part 2, 1.12.1883, p. 1014; Part 3, 8.12.1883, p. 1072; Part 4, 15.12,1883, p. 1113; Part 5, 22.12,1883, p. 1160.
11 Ernest Favenc, "Diary of Expedition in Northern Territory from Powell's Creek to Daly Waters. May 28–Jy 15, 1883". Mitchell Library ML B 879.
12 Peter Donovan, *A Land Full of Possibilities: A History of South Australia's Northern Territory*, St. Lucia: University of Queendsland Press, 1981, p. 130.

"First Pastoral Settlement in Northern Territory". Under the heading "First Lady Explorer", Giles wrote: "To-day, 20th June 1883, Mr. and Mrs. Creaghe came to Springvale. They are members of Mr. Ernest Favenc's exploring expedition. They have come on ahead from Powell's Creek, where they left Messrs. Favenc and Lindsay Crawford to finish the exploration. Mrs. Creaghe has ridden the whole distance on horseback and is undoubtedly the first lady to tackle exploring in Australia."[13]

Favenc's detour to the McArthur was a long and arduous journey – having left Powell's Creek on 28 May, he did not reach his nominated destination, Daly Waters, until 15 July. When they were finally reunited with the Creaghes on 26 July, Caroline reported that they still appeared very thin. That gathering was short-lived. Favenc's brief completed, he left just two days later, returning south via Darwin. The Creaghes followed a few days later, on 3 August, in the company of the Giles, their Chinese cook and an indigenous stockman. They reached Darwin on 14 August, from where they departed to Sydney on the 22nd aboard the "Feilung".

The Legacy of Caroline Creaghe

Diaries are by their nature private documents, and Caroline Creaghe's is no exception. It tells us a lot about the remarkable woman who carried it over several months, and who somehow, in most cases after the rigours of a day's travel, could still find the energy to record the events of the day. It also tells us much about her relations, first and foremost with her beloved and ill-fated husband Harry, but also with the other members of the expedition, and with the people they met along the way.

But this diary is much more than a record of Caroline Creaghe's experiences through the better part of the year 1883. It records and preserves for us well over a century later the realities of exploration in parts of Australia which remained the least well

---

13 Alfred Giles, "First Pastoral Settlement in Northern Territory", in *The North Queensland Register*, 9 January 1932. A typescript of the article is held with the Diary of Caroline Creaghe in the Mitchell Library.

known. Above all, it does so from the most unusual perspective of a woman, and one blessed with the literary talent to describe the daily struggles which all had to endure. The diary thus offers compelling insights into the travails of nineteenth century land exploration:– the harshness of the northern climate, the permanent shortage of food, the ongoing struggle to find adequate water for humans and horses alike, the constant harassment by flies and mosquitoes, and the exhaustion of constant travel. Moreover, punctuated as her expedition was by sometimes lengthy stays at a number of stations, the diary conveys to the modern reader a clear sense of the hardships and privations of everyday life endured in the remote north by those who had chosen to settle there. And although Caroline herself was not to remain there in the longer term, her diary depicts the reality of sustained isolation which afflicted both women and men.

Distinctive though it is for its woman's perspective, the diary is nonetheless in many regards a document of its times. This is especially evident in Caroline's reporting of relations with indigenous Australians, to whom she characteristically refers as "blacks" or even "niggers". In 1883, and in both North Queensland and in the Northern Territory, race relations were in a vexed state. That acts of violence occurred is well known from the historical record and is evident from Creaghe's diary as well. She reports, for example, the killing of the pastoralist Crawford. Perhaps even more revealing, though, in the diary, is the brooding sense of fear, occasionally acute and never fully discarded, which accompanied the expeditioners. It persuaded them to travel by day with fire-arms at the ready, to sleep with loaded revolvers under their pillows and a carbine Snider at the tent entrance at night, and to remain ever watchful, fearing an attack at any moment.

In reality Creaghe had little direct contact with indigenous people in the course of the expedition; indeed in places it might be inferred that the latter took measures to avoid direct contact but simply to observe the interlopers. As the Favenc expedition consisted of just three men and a woman, accompanied by horses but no cattle whatsoever, and as its members did not behave in an overtly violent manner, the Aborigines may well have viewed it quite differently from the overlanding expeditions of that era. Nonetheless, the diary makes it quite clear that at that time the pastoralists' efforts to assert control over large tracts of territory, and the Aborigines' determination to resist them, had led to a state of violence, especially where settlement was already well advanced in parts of North Queensland. Not surprisingly given the superiority of European weapons, hostilities led to the loss of a disproportionately large number of indigenous lives.

Beyond acknowledging the frightful reality of this fatal frontier violence, the diary also draws attention to the blatantly exploitative relationships which existed at other levels, such as those between master and servant or slave. Intriguingly for a document of its time, the diary also conveys a sense of understanding and sympathy for the Aborigines' dilemma. After an encounter with a group of them who, Creaghe speculates, had never before seen Europeans, she reports, "The poor things were quiet and frightened." Later on the evening of the same day she reflects with admirable insight that "harm has been done so often by white men stealing Blacks' only means of gaining their food."

Race relations of other kinds too are touched upon. Not only North Queensland but the Northern Territory also had a sizeable population of Chinese, especially as a result of the gold rush which had begun in 1872. Many of them, as Creaghe notes, found their way into domestic service. Given Creaghe's own Indian colonial background this must have seemed a not unusual state of affairs, though in places like the Palmerston of the 1880s the relative numbers of non-Europeans must have been quite confronting. Against that, Palmerston could also offer some of the comforts of civilized life:– a church, tennis, a piano, and a round of social engagements with those who constituted the Establishment of the day.

Alas, none of this was sufficient to draw Caroline back to the far North. As the Afterword shows, her future lay elsewhere. More happily, however, Caroline's diary allows us to travel back to Australia's North, both in space and in time, and helps us explore a world which we too might find challenging and strange.

THE DIARY OF EMILY CAROLINE CREAGHE, EXPLORER

Left Sydney in the "Corea" on Saturday 23rd December. Had a long passage of 66 hours to Brisbane. Arrived at 8 o'clock in the morning of Boxing Day. Went to Goodna[1] by the 12 train & were met by Papa (to our surprise) in the phaeton.[2] Found Louie[3] & Miss Sharpe well & happy. Left Brisbane on Thursday at 1/2 past 7 P.M. Arrived at Rockhampton (Keppel Bay) at 1/2 past 7 P.M. on Saturday 30th. Anchored in the Bay for an hour or two to take cargo. Not time to go ashore. Could see nothing of the town. Left for Bowen at 9 P.M. Raining all New Year's Eve. (46 miles from R'ton)[4]

1 Monday, January

Arrived at Bowen at 10 A.M. Saw black fellows in their canoes in a state of nudity for the first time. Canoes are made of sheets of bark, paddled with one oar in the bows. A woman amused us for some time by diving for money the passengers threw into the sea for her. We went on shore after luncheon & saw all over the town. There are about 2 or 300 houses, none at all large, & very much scattered. One street wide, but evidently not much used, as grass is growing in abundance about it. As it is New Year's day we cannot see what sort of shops there are, but for the same reason no cargo has been discharged, so the steamer is delayed till tomorrow, & we can see the town again under ordinary circumstances before we start. We went into a black woman's cottage & bought a few shells for a 1/- for Mrs. Ward. Most of the natives live outside the town in caves and bark tents. Half of the people about today were blacks. It has been raining in showers all day, but the soil is so sandy that it is not muddy.

---

1 Township just west of Brisbane where Caroline and Harry met. They married in nearby Ipswich.
2 Phaeton – an open four-wheeled carriage normally drawn by two horses.
3 Possibly Caroline's stepmother Eliza Francis.
4 These words in parentheses were added in pencil. R'ton is Rockhampton.

2 Tuesday

Left Bowen at breakfast time. Did not go on shore again. Fine day. Arrived at Townsville at 1/2 past 9 P.M. Anchored in the bay about 8 miles out from the town. Remained on board all night. Mangoes grow in abundance, & cocoa-nuts also. The town consists of one road (like a piece of a paddock with some shops on either side) it is so rough & grass is growing so well over it. Arrived at Townsville too late to go on shore. Anchored out in the bay.

3 Wednesday

Went on shore in a dirty little steamer at 1/2 past 6 A.M. Went with the Bauers to the Queen's Hotel to breakfast, splendid hotel. Saw all over the town & went back to luncheon. Went back to "Corea" at 6 o'clock. Left Townsville at 1/2 past 8 P.M. Fine weather. Was agreeably surprised at seeing such a large town. Fruits – mangoes, tamarinds, immense pineapples, paupau apples & melons & bananas. Townsville has one long street with rather nice shops & offices on either side. Very warm.

4 Thursday

Fine day, arrived & anchored in the Bay, about half a mile from the few stones piled up called a wharf at Port Douglas. Too late to go ashore. Fished & got numbers of small fish. Miss Bauer & a few of us went into the cook's galley & cleaned & cooked them. Heavy tropical shower of rain in the evening. Getting very hot.

5 Friday

At P. Douglas

Went ashore in a little boat and "did" the town. A long street going right down to the beach with stores on both sides. Intensely hot, scarcely a breath of air. Had some tea & bread & butter at the best of the hotels up in a wide balcony where it was a shade cooler. Left Port Douglas at 5 o'clock. No Churches of any denomination north of Townsville.

6 Saturday

Arrived at Cooktown at 2 or 3 A.M. Came to the wharf at daylight. Bauers left the "Corea". Went on shore after breakfast. Small town similar to the others, with one long street. Shops (or "stores" rather) slightly better than those at Port Douglas & Bowen on either side. One side is almost entirely taken up by chinese. Mostly a chinese population seemingly. Almost all chinese servants. Went to see the Bauers at the hotel they were at. Public houses predominate throughout the town. The same trees and fruits as at the other ports. Went for a walk with Harry in the afternoon round the rocks. Left the wharf at about midnight. All the passengers for Thursday island were most awfully tipsy. It speaks badly for the inhabitants of the place. Intensely hot –

7 Sunday

Beautiful weather; very hot. Stopped at Channel island Light-ship for a few minutes to give them some provisions & their mail. Four men belonging to the Lightship came for them in a boat. Passed Lizard Island the place where Mrs. Watson was attacked by the blacks, also the island where she died from want of water.[5] The second steward had an epileptic fit at dinner time.

8 Monday

Fine Weather. Anchored at 3 A.M. at Claremont Lightship. Went on at daylight. Remained at Pt. Piper Light-ship for an hour or so at tea time. Our last night in the "Corea". Anchored a mile or two from Pt.

---

5   Lizard Island was so named by Captain Cook because of the abundance of lizards there. The ill-fated Mary Watson and her husband Bob became inhabitants of the island in 1880 when they established a small fishing station there for the purpose of catching bêche-de-mer. The island was occasionally visited by indigenous people, though only by initiated males. In 1881 Bob Watson left Mary, their newborn and two Chinese servants on the island, while he went in search of more productive fishing grounds. After the death of one of her Chinese servants and the wounding of the other, Mary elected to try to leave the island with her baby and the wounded servant. Their vessel was a converted iron tank, normally used for boiling bêche-de-mer. They died of thirst after the vessel had reached another island, Howick Island No. 5; the bodies – of Mary, baby Ferrier and Ah Sam – were recovered in January 1882. For a full treatment of the story see Jillian Robertson, *Lizard Island: A Reconstruction of the Life of Mrs Watson*, Melbourne: Hutchinson, 1981.

~~Piper Lightship during a severe thunder storm at about 8 o'clock P.M. Entered the Albany Pass at 1/2 past 12 o'clock, arrived at Thursday island at about 1/2 past 4. Mr. Favenc came in Capt. Chester's boat to meet us & brought us up to his house to stay for the few days we shall be here. Mrs. Chester is not at home.~~[6]

9 Tuesday

~~Fine day until 8 o'clock this evening when a severe thunder storm came, and we were. Mr.~~[7] Entered Albany Pass at noon & arrived at Thursday Island at 1/2 past 4 this afternoon. Mr. Favenc came to meet us in Capt. Chester's boat & brought us to his house where he wants us to remain for the few days we are on the island. Mrs. Chester is away from home. One son is at home. Met here a Mr. Russel an old acquaintance of Charlie's,[8] he is going down south tomorrow, so will see Charlie and tell him of us.

10 Wednesday

Very hot. Did nothing particular. Went for a walk with Harry & Mrs. Favenc in the afternoon. No churches of any description. The drinking that goes on in this little place is something tremendous.

11 Thursday

The "Almora" arrived from home this morning, and all the gentlemen went off on board, and would not take us so we (Mrs. Favenc & I) went over in Mr. Booer's boat and spent the day with them. We all went for a sail to Capt. Tucker's Pearl Station in the afternoon, and to serve Mr. Favenc and Harry right did not come back until late in the evening. They had been rather nervous about us, so were relieved to see us home safely.

---

6   The section beginning "Anchored a mile or two . . ." and ending ". . . not at home" has been crossed out in the original. Other deletions in the original, providing they remain legible, are dealt with similarly.

7   As above.

8   Charlie – Charles James Robinson – was Caroline's brother, older by some seven years.

12 Friday
Did nothing particular. The "Merkara" came in from Brisbane & Mr. Chester brought the Captain & 3 of the passengers to spend the evening. Went for a walk in the morning with Harry round the rocks.

13 Saturday
Went in Mr. Chester's boat with Harry & Mr. & Mrs. Favenc at 1/2 past 5 A.M. to the Booers at Prince of Wales island (just opposite to Thursday island). Returned at about 11 & packed. Left for Normanton at 4 P.M. in the "Truganini". Fine Weather.

14 Sunday
Fine weather until late in the evening, when we had a heavy thunder storm & we all got drenched, as we were sleeping. Out of sight of land all day.

15 Monday
Fine weather, but seem to be going into the rainy season at Normanton. Still out of sight of land.

16 Tuesday
Arrived at "The Flinders" a telegraph station at the mouth of the Norman river, about 30 miles from Normanton. Anchored a few hundred yards from the beach, & took the ship's boat & went on shore, to pick up shells of which there were any quantity. Nothing to be seen. No houses but the telegraph station. Level country. Left the Flinders at 3 P.M. & arrived at some islands called Baffle group at 8 P.M. about 3 quarters of the way up the river. Anchored there to wait for the steamer to take us on to Normanton.

17 Wednesday
Came up to Normanton in a steam launch. The trip from the "Truganini" took about an hour & a half. Mr. Forsyth mgr. Burns Philp[9]

---

9   The clarification "mgr. Burns Philp" was added in ink. The firm "Burns, Philp and Co." was founded in April 1883 when the interests of James Burns and Robert Philp were merged. The registered office was in Sydney, but the main mercantile and shipping interests at that time were in the far north, in such places

came to meet us & brought us (Harry & me) to their house to stay. Mr. & Mrs. Favenc went to Mr. Bedfords'. Normanton is a level township with about 300 inhabitants. No churches of any denomination. Fine weather still.

18 Thursday

Found today that Mrs. Favenc is not strong enough to go out to the exploring expedition, so, much to our disgust, we have to give up all idea of going. She is going back to Sydney with Mr. Favenc & I am going to Mr. Shadforth's station 220 miles inland with Harry. When Mr. Favenc returns in March, the two will go out with one man, & get the work done in 3 months instead of 4 1/2 as they would have done if we had gone. Harry took me to see the Bedfords this afternoon.

19 Friday

Did nothing particular. We all went to the Bedfords' after tea. We start tomorrow for the Shadforths'. Fine weather.

20 Saturday

Left Normanton at 1/2 past 3 P.M. for "Magowrah" Mr. Trimbel's station, a distance of 16 miles. Arrived there at 7. About a dozen men camped all night, and 8 of us belonging to the party going inland. Mr. Shadforth, Mr. Murray, McNaught, Power, two men & ourselves. Being the only female except one in the kitchen, I felt decidedly queer amongst such a number of men.

21 Sunday

Left Magowrah at 9 A.M. passed the Bynoe river, Flinders river & had dinner at Armstrong creek. The men left almost immediately after dinner for L creek a distance of 32 miles. Called after

---

as Townsville, Normanton, Burketown and Thursday Island. The two vessels on which Creaghe travelled, the "Corea" and the "Truganini", were operated by Burns Philp, the "Truganini" in particular being used to run mail between Thursday Island and Normanton. For a history of the company see K. Buckley and K. Klugman, *The History of Burns Philp: The Australian Company in the South Pacific*, n.p.: Burns, Philp & Co., 1981.

Leichardt[10] the explorer, whose initials are on a tree on the bank of the creak. I felt nearly done up when we got to Armstrong creak, having come 16 miles & not yet being accustomed to long rides and poor food,[11] but managed to get to the end of the second stage, but was nearly knocked up. Got into camp at 1/2 past 7 P.M. Rather hot. Scarcely anything but bare plains all the way.

22 Monday

Made a start at about 1/2 past 6 A.M. Arrived at camp a mile & a half this side of M Lagoon 22 miles from L creak, Called after Morrel, Leichardt's companion at about noon. We (Harry & I) did intend remaining in camp at L creak all today, as I am nearly "finished", but there is every appearance of rain, so we must push on to cross the River Leichardt before it is flooded. The hottest weather I have ever felt today. The flies are something dreadful. Mr. McNaught & his man left the camp in the afternoon. Still the country level & bare.

23 Tuesday

Left M Lagoon at 1/2 past 6 A.M. Passed Diary Creek and camped on Pack Saddle Creek where the mosquitoes were something terrible. Two men came up going to Normanton & camped with us, but were driven away at last by the mosquitoes at 3 A.M. Mr. Shadforth left us for a few days to call at Burktown[12] & will catch us up again. Mr. Power left with him, so only 4 of us are left. Diary creek gets its name from an old diary being found there, "Packsaddle" from an old saddle being found there, both articles supposed to have belonged to Leichardt's party. Nicely timbered country.

---

10 Creaghe's mis-spelling of "Leichhardt". As discussed in the Introduction, the German explorer Ludwig Leichhardt undertook a successful expedition from southern Queensland to Port Essington in the years 1844–45. For part of its journey in the vicinity of the Gulf of Carpentaria Creaghe's party covered territory explored by Leichhardt nearly four decades earlier.
11 The section beginning "& not yet being ..." was added in ink on the blotter.
12 Actually Burketown.

24 Wednesday

Left Packsaddle at 1/2 past 8 A.M. The horses got away & the men were from 1/2 past 5 looking for them. Travelled all the morning. Passed Margaret Lagoon & are now camped on the banks of the River Leichardt. There is an old tumbled down public house close to the river crossing. The country is again plains, & not much timber. The heat is intense. No rain yet, but every appearance of it. Yesterday we did about 20 miles, & today about 18. There are plenty of aligators in the river but I have not seen one yet. Warner had a fearful headache when we got to camp, we hope he has not had a touch of the sun.[13]

25 Thursday

Left the Leichardt camp at 7 A.M. & arrived at "The Rocky" at 1/2 past 10 a distance of 14 or 15 miles. Warner, (Mr. Murray's man) who had not been well last night got some terrible fits, & has evidently had a sunstroke. He managed to drive the pack horses into camp, but got ill immediately on arrival. Mr. Watson & two men from his station 12 miles distant came up, & he being a friend of Harry's stopped all day & night with us. He gave us an account of his being speared by the blacks some little time ago. He was of great assistance in helping to hold Warner in the fits. We are afraid he won't get over it, as he is still unconscious.

26 Friday

A plague of beetles last night! Warner is slightly better, & has not had a return of the fits, but our going any further this morning is quite out of the question. We did not put up the tents last night for the first time, as it looked so very unlike rain, & it was too hot to sleep in it, so when a thunder storm broke in the middle of the night we all had to turn out & put them up as fast as we could & only just put the finishing touches when down it came. Mr. Watson went off before we were up. It is fine & very hot today. (Evening) Warner is much worse this evening. He is quite unconscious, & has been since 10 A.M. It is most painful to hear his groans. A terrific thunder storm at 8 this evening, got a little wet.

---

13 The last sentence has been added.

27 Saturday

Warner died at 3 this morning. He never became conscious. His groans were something terrible all night. Poor Mr. Murray sat with him. A death in a camping party is an awful thing. Mr. Murray went away at 7 A.M. to Augustus Downs[14] & brought back Mr. Watson & two men with pick & shovel to dig a grave. Harry & I spent a miserable day until 1/2 past 3 by ourselves in camp guarding the body from native dogs. They have just sewn up his body in his blanket in the midst of a heavy thunder storm, while some of the others are digging the grave. The poor fellow was quite a young fellow, strong, tall & healthy 3 days ago. "In the midst of life we are in death". Mr. Watson & men will camp all night with us. We shall leave early tomorrow morning. Mr. Watson brought us some milk, bread & plain cake & a watermelon which were great treats. At least the milk was. I have got into that state from not eating, that I could not manage even cake. Our food in camp consists of nasty, dirty, hairy, dried salt beef, dark brown sugar (half dust) & hard dry damper. There are some tinned meats, but the jolting has made them uneatable. There is some jam, but who can eat it with hard, dry damper, no butter.

28 Sunday

They finished the grave at 2 A.M. & so poor Warner was buried in the dead of night. The horses were troublesome, so we did not start till 20 to 9 this morning. Only went 7 miles, as the heat became so intense it was dangerous to travel. Camped till 5 o'clock at the side of a waterhole. Travelled until 1/2 past 8 & then camped at The Ridgepoll on Fiery Creek, about 19 miles from The Rocky. The food we are living upon is something horrible. I have scarcely touched a thing since we left Normanton; just two or three mouthfuls at each meal, but make up for the want of food, by drinking any amount of tea (without milk) which is detestable.

---

14 Augustus Downs homestead is situated a short distance east of the Leichhardt River.

29 Monday

Left the Ridge poll at 7 A.M. & did not camp till we reached Topwater, Cartridge Creek at 12, noon, having ridden about 22 miles. We took the wrong track from "The Bucket" so had about 5 miles of a round. Left Top water at 1/2 past 4 & arrived at "Gregory Downs" (a station belonging to Watson bros.) at 8. The shanty consists of one room (in the main building) with an earth floor, forms to sit upon, & two rough stretchers in two corners. Stores, etc, are piled up all over the room. However bad as it is I was very glad to have tea there. Nothing to eat but tinned fishes & bread, with a tin billy for teapot, & pannikins to drink out of. There are several other travellers camping for the night here. We have our tent pitched a short way from the house.

30 Tuesday

Left Gregory Downs after breakfast and camped in the heat of the day at the old Police camp, by the side of the Gregory River; such a pretty river, with Palm trees & pandanas growing on either side, the water is as clear as crystal running over pebbles. Left at 4 & camped for the night at an old copper mine which two men worked at some years ago, & gave up as a bad job. Travelled about 20 miles.

31 Wednesday

Left Copper Mine at 1/4 to 7 A.M. & camped at L tree[15] in the middle of the day. Travelled on again at 4, & came across the mountains during a severe thunder storm, & arrived at Carl Creek (the Shadforths' station), at 1/2 past 7 or 8, heartily glad to get to the end of my journey. How I do wish Harry had a billet in town instead of having to "rough it" like this. Did about 25 miles in all.

---

15 The tree in question might have been scored with the letter "L" by Leichhardt. An overlander named George De Lautour also marked trees at his campsites with an "L". For this information I am indebted to Tony Roberts.

Thursday Island Torres Strait 1887, by H.G. Lloyd.
State Library of New South Wales

Frank Hann an explorer with Talbot ca. 1890
Battye Library Perth

1 Thursday

They are all early risers here, so we were up soon after daylight, & breakfasted before 7. The household consists of Mr. & Mrs. Shadforth and 10 children, only 6 of whom are at home just now. The house is a log one partitioned off into 4 rooms with no ceilings, so that the slightest whisper can be heard all over it. ~~It is a shade better than camping out, & that is all I can say for it.~~ Very hot. No flies or mosquitoes. There are two black gins as servants, but most of the work falls on Mrs. Shadforth & the girls.

2 Friday

Mr. Bob Shadforth came home today & brought Mr. Willie Taylor with him. Gentlemen seem to call in pretty constantly on their way out to their stations. Very hot. We had a thunder storm in the afternoon. The principal amusement is bathing. The river runs a few yards from the house, so I & the two girls go in 2 & 3 times during the day, & were not in the least deterred by the sight of crocodiles watching us on the bank near by, as this particular species are not man eaters.[16]

3 Saturday

In the afternoon Mr. Doyle who has a station about a mile from here brought 3 horses & took us for a ride & Mr. Lamond (Miss Shadforth's fiancée) the Inspector of the Native police,[17] camped about 2 miles from here. They both returned for the evening. The mailman arrived from Normanton going up as far as "Rocklands", he will be back on his way back to Normanton in 6 or 7 days.

---

16 The section from "& were not in the least ..." has been added in pencil.
17 Native Police corps existed in various parts of Australia from as early as 1837. In Queensland, which had become a separate colony in 1859, the Native Mounted Police were commonly referred to as the Black Police. Typically the officers were Europeans, the troops indigenous. The small frontier detachments gained a reputation for violence, especially in actions against indigenous people euphemistically called "dispersals". South Australia, which in Creaghe's time was the colony responsible for the Northern Territory, had had a Native Police Force for a time in the 1850s, but it was not until 1884 – and just after Creaghe's expedition – that a Northern Territory version of the Native Police was founded. See *The Encyclopaedia of Aboriginal Australia*, ed. David Horton, Canberra: Aboriginal Studies Press, 1994, pp. 765–66.

4 Sunday

There is scarcely any difference made between this and any other day.[18] Mr. Shadforth wanted to finish putting up our bed (as yet we have been sleeping on the floor not boarded) but I begged him not to, so to please me he desisted. They generally go out for a ride, but I suppose having been yesterday, they did not think of it today. Mr. Murray went on to his station "Morston"[19] this morning.

5 Monday

Did nothing particular. Mr. Lamb a young fellow camped some distance from here arrived from Normanton.

6 Tuesday

Did nothing particular. Miss Shadforth & I helped the gins to wash all the morning. It was very hot. No rain yet. The washing is all taken down to the bank of the creek & boiled in kerosene tins.[20]

7 Wednesday

Intensely hot today, I never felt anything like the heat. I do miss the fruits and vegetables. There is no such luxury up here. Mr. Lamb left this morning. Last night we brought our blankets out onto the verandah, it was too hot to be indoors. Ironed all the afternoon.

8 Thursday

We slept again outside, but even then it was too hot to sleep. Mr. Bob Shadforth went up to "Lorne hill"[21] Mr. Jack Watson's and Mr. Frank Hann's[22] station about 40 miles away. Very Hot. No Rain. Mr. Watson has 40 pairs of blacks' ears nailed round the walls collected during raiding parties after the loss of many cattle speared by the blacks.[23]

---

18 Creaghe regarded Sunday as a day of rest.
19 Morstone was some 70 kilometres north-north-east of Camooweal.
20 The last sentence was added in pencil.
21 Lawn Hill Station.
22 The section "& Mr. Frank Hann's" was added in pencil.
23 The last sentence was added in pencil. Deborah Bird Rose has described Jack Watson as "one of the most violent men on the northern frontier in the 1880s

9 Friday
Did nothing particular. Still no rain, very hot.

10 Saturday
Very hot, still no rain. Mr. Bob Shadforth came back from Lorne Hill.

11 Sunday
The mailman came, & went on South. Wrote to Papa & Jessie.[24]

12 Monday
Mrs. Shadforth was unwell all day. Did some washing in the morning. Very hot. Mr. Shadforth went down to meet his son Ernest who is coming from Bourktown with the provisions in a dray; he ought to have been here today, so he is a little anxious about him. Bourktown is 4 or 5 days journey from here & the blacks are particularly aggresive in the district.[25]

13 Tuesday
Washed again this morning & ironed this afternoon. No-one but Mr. Lamond has been here for some time. Miss Shadforth is going to be married in May, so she, Mrs. Shadforth & Bob will have to go to Normanton then. They will be taking a buggy, so Harry says I may go too then & wait at Mrs. Forsyth's until he comes, instead of remaining here, I am so glad only 3 months more! No rain, intensely hot. I still sleep on the verandah. That is too hot even for Harry, he takes his blankets right outside.

---

and 90s. [...] Watson had a reputation for being 'hard on the blacks', as they called it then. In 1895 he became manager of Victoria River Downs station, remaining there until his death the next year." Deborah Bird Rose, "Aboriginal life and death in Australian settler nationhood", *Aboriginal History* 25 (2001), p. 149.

24 Jessie Robinson, Caroline's older sister by some 9 years.
25 The section from "& blacks are ..." was added in pencil.

14 Wednesday

Nothing happened of any consequence. Trying to exist through the great heat of both day and night.

15 Thursday

A nice cool wind sprang up during the night, & the sun is not so strong, so it is pleasantly cool today. It looks a little like rain. Mr. Lamond brought his express over & took us to the Native Police encampment. It consists of about 15 bark humpies round a square courtyard. There are several gins with their picininies,[26] all with no clothing on. Mr. Lamond's abode is only a log hut divided into four compartments.

16 Friday

It was showery all night but today the rain has ceased, but it is still cloudy. Amy Shadforth, Edith & I went for a walk to the Tarpaean rock about 2 miles from here. We called in at Mr. Doyle's humpie on our way. His place is a little inferior to this. Mr. Russel a brother of the one we met at Thursday island, arrived at about 1/2 past 8, this evening.

17 Saturday

It rained on & off all last night, then a little showery all day. Mr. Tudor Shadforth, the second son, came from the station he is on this evening, to stay till Monday.

18 Sunday

There have been a few showers today. Mr. Doyle came to tea & spent the evening. Went for a short stroll with Harry in the afternoon. Mr. Lamond & little Harry came over this evening as usual. Harry Shadforth about 10 years old lives with his future brother in law.[27]

---

26 Children.
27 The last sentence was added in pencil.

19 Monday
Raining pretty heavily in showers all day. The air is delightfully cool.

20 Tuesday
The rainy season seems to have set in, in real good earnest; it has been raining heavily nearly all day. Mr. Shadforth & Ernest Shadforth came home, but had to leave the dray at Gregory Downs as the roads were too heavy & the rivers too high. They brought a new black gin with them; she cannot speak a word of English. Mr. Shadforth put a rope round the gin's neck & dragged her along on foot, he was riding. This seems to be the usual method.[28]

21 Wednesday
No rain this morning, but dull & cloudy. Rained all the afternoon in showers. The new gin, whom they call Bella, is chained up to a tree a few yards from the house, she is not to be loosed until they think she is tamed.

22 Thursday
Showery in the morning, but poured with rain all the afternoon and all night. The river close to this house has not risen yet, but the others must be flooded by this time.

23 Friday
It poured all last night, and it is still raining this morning. Rained hard all the afternoon, but only slightly through the night. The new gin made Topsey (an old one) jealous, & the latter threw a fire-stick at her & said she would kill her. The stick flew past Mrs. Shadforth's face so Madame Topsey got a thrashing.

24 Saturday
Bella, the new gin, decamped in the night, whether it was because of Topsey's threat to kill her, or discontent at this life we don't know. They tracked her as far as the O'Shanassy, but that river is a "banker", so they could not go after her any further. It rained a little this

---

28 The section beginning "Mr. Shadforth put a rope . . ." was added in pencil.

morning, but all the afternoon it has been fine. A few showers have fallen this evening. There is no mail expected for 2 months on account of the floods.

25 Sunday

Scarcely any rain fell today.

26 Monday

No rain to speak of today.

27 Tuesday

No rain at all, the rain seems clearing away. If no more wet weather comes before next week Harry & Mr. Bob will go on down to the Norman. The air is so nice & pure.

28 Wednesday

Harry & Mr. Lamond took we three girls for a ride this afternoon. We went 8 or 10 miles in all. First to see a number of Palm Trees & then to the O'Shannassy to see how high it had risen. It is low again now, but it has been very high from all appearances. Delightfully cool.

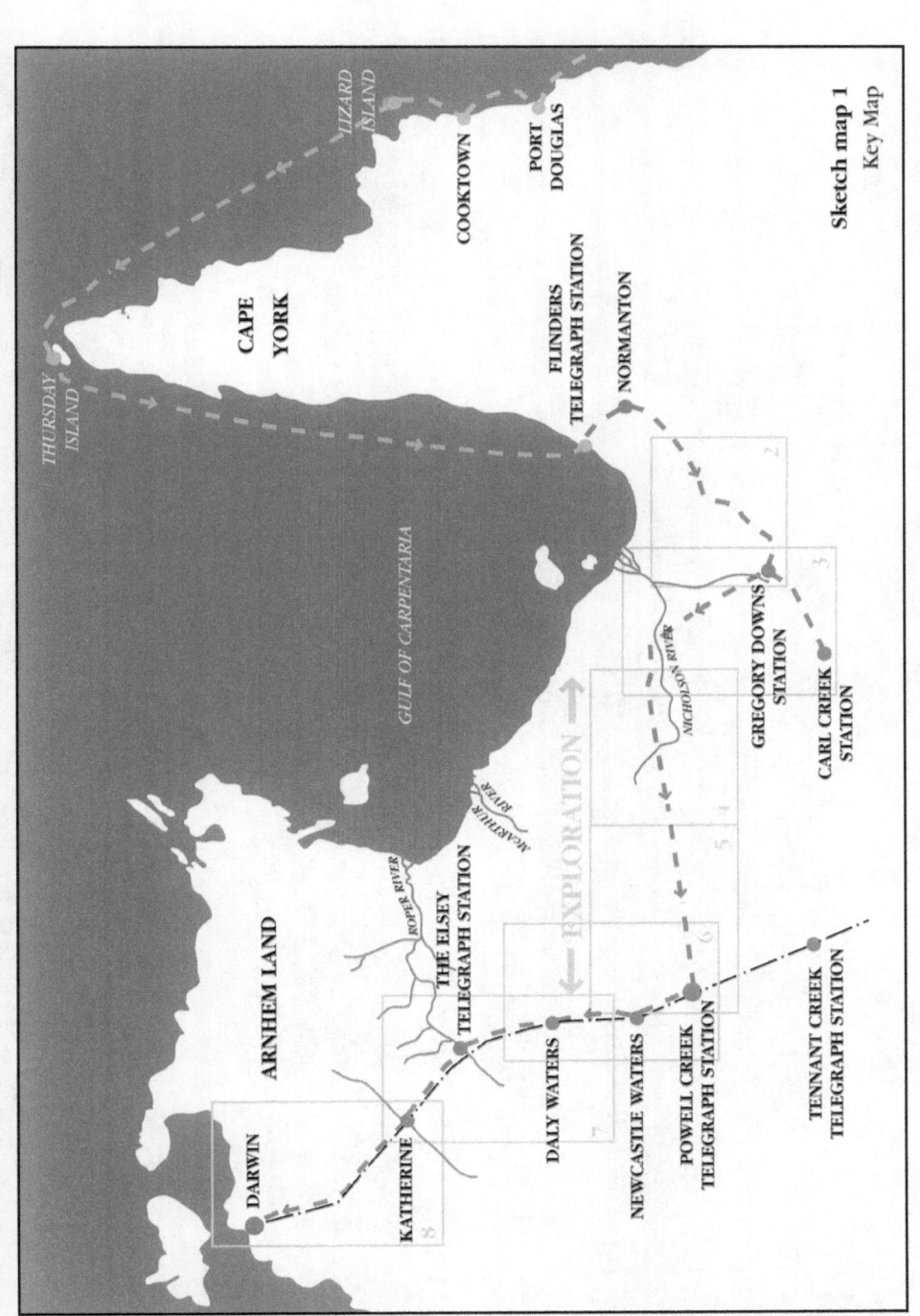

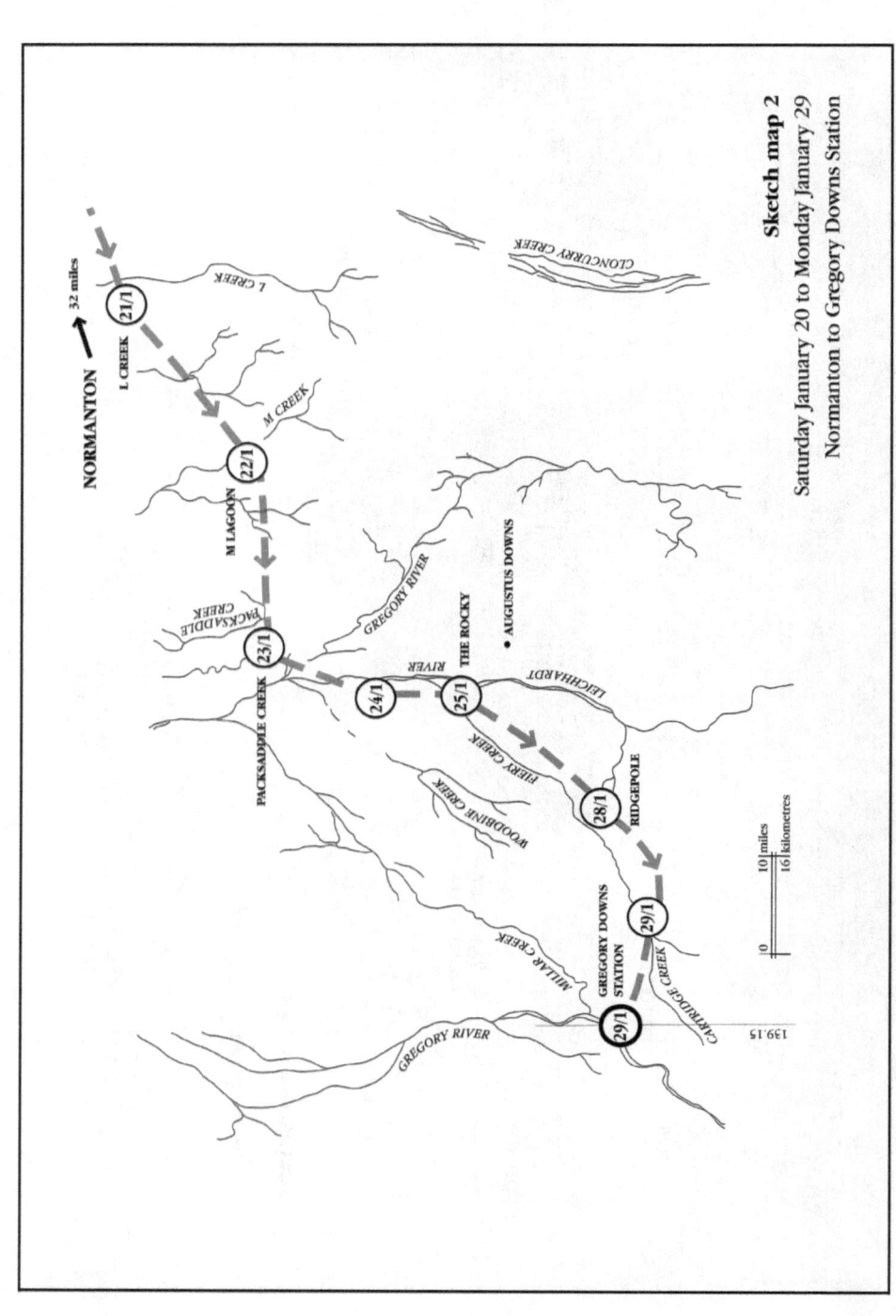

Sketch map 2
Saturday January 20 to Monday January 29
Normanton to Gregory Downs Station

1 Thursday

The time is drawing close for Harry to go away & no more rain has come to postpone it. Harry & I went for one of our short strolls along the river bank. The flies are too bad for the walks to be enjoyable. It is nice and cool still.

2 Friday

Mr. Shadforth & Mr. Bob went out on the "Run" today & will be away until tomorrow. Harry was to have gone but he was unwell all day so could not.

3 Saturday

Mr. Willis came this afternoon from his station 12 or 14 miles away "Margaret Vale" the one Mr. Tudor is on.[29] Mr. Shadforth returned this evening after tea, & Mr. Bob turned up earlier in the day.

4 Sunday

Mrs. Shadforth, the girls, Mr. Willis, Mr. Doyle & Mr. Lamond & all the children went for a ride & drive calling in at the police camp on their way. It being Sunday, I did not go. Harry & I went for a walk by ourselves. Wrote to Minnie.[30]

5 Monday

Mr. Watson and Mr. Han[31] from Lorne Hill came this afternoon. They pitched their tent a short distance from the house, but had tea with us. Mr. Han owns Lorne Hill Station (cattle) and Mr. Jack Watson manages in his absence. Wrote to Lilla[32] & Papa.

---

29 That is, Mr Tudor Shadforth.
30 Mary Robinson, Caroline's younger sister by 5 years.
31 Hann. Frank Hann (1846–1921) was a prominent pastoralist. He and Edward Edkins had re-established Lawn Hill Station in 1875. Hann remained there until 1895, by which time the station had been seized by the Bank of New South Wales. Information courtesy of Tony Roberts.
32 Harriet Eliza Emma Robinson, Caroline's eldest sister, born in 1849. Her husband was Dr William Lamb, who was mdeical superintendent of Goodna Hospital. It was there that Caroline met Harry, a patient, when she was visting Lilla.

6 Tuesday

Mr. Han & Mr. Watson had breakfast here, left soon after. Clouds seem gathering up again. If it rains before Thursday, Harry and Mr. Bob will have to postpone their departure. As Harry will have to go sometime, I hope he will get away on Thursday as the sooner he goes the sooner we shall get back to Sydney & then I hope most sincerely there will be no more partings. I washed and ironed nearly all the morning and afternoon. Mr. Lamond went out on patrol, he will be away a fortnight.

7 Wednesday

Fine weather still. Went for a walk this afternoon along the river bank with Harry, and again this evening towards the crossing. Our last stroll together until we return together to the Norman. I am not going down with Amy, but will wait here for Harry, as Mrs. Shadforth will feel more comfortable at my being with Edith, when she is away. Mr. Shadforth went to Gregory Downs to bring on the dray which Ernie had to leave before the wet.

8 Thursday

Poor old Harry went away today with Mr. Bob at 3 or 4 this afternoon. I hope he will be back in 12 weeks, I wonder if <u>he will</u>! He was dreadfully "cut up" about leaving me, of <u>course</u> I was, & am. The weather is getting very hot again. Clouds still are gathering but no rain yet. No men on the place but Mr. Taylor. It seems so strange & dull.

9 Friday

We had a short but heavy thunderstorm this afternoon, not enough to cool the air for more than an hour or two after the rain had ceased. Doing needlework all day.

10 Saturday

Working all day at a dress for Edith, trying to make the hours fly by. We are all beginning to mope, having no gentlemen in the evenings. We go to bed almost directly after tea, not knowing what else to do. It is too hot and the insects are too numerous for us to sit & work or read indoors, so after a half an hour or so sitting in the dark on the verandah, we one by one retire to our beds. Very hot all day.

11 Sunday

Six years today since Mamma died! Harry will get to the Leichardt sometime during the day I expect. (Evening) Such a long day I never spent. We came to bed at 1/2 past 7, glad at last to have reached the close of the day.

12 Monday

Mr. Shadforth came back, having left the dray bogged 8 miles from here. He will go with Mr. Taylor tomorrow to dig it out. It was a relief to see him ride up, we were all so dull. It was a little cooler today. Mr. Shadforth saw Harry & Mr. Bob 10 miles this side of Gregory Downs. They were well & getting on all right.

13 Tuesday

Mr. Shadforth and Mr. Taylor left this morning at about 1/2 past 12 to bring the dray but could not get further than the police camp before dark. Mr. T. came home to sleep, but Mr. Shadforth is remaining at the camp.

14 Wednesday

Mr. Murray came & brought Ernie from Margaret Vale in his buggy. Mr. Willis's house on that station was burnt to the ground a day or two ago, & all their personal effects. The store is safe fortunately. They were all out on the Run while it happened. Mr. Shadforth brought the dray early this morning, so Edith & I unpacked all the stores.

15 Thursday

Very hot all day, we did nothing particular. Worked. Ernie, Mr. Murray & we 3 girls had a dance at the back of the house after tea.

16 Friday

Mr. Murray, Mr. Ernie, Edith & I went for a ride to the "Basin" about 5 miles away. Coming back, Ernie & I rode over a big brown snake, they tried to find & kill it, but it had disappeared. Mr. Willis came from Margaret Vale at about 1/2 past 7 in the evening. Mr. Tudor Shadforth is ill with fever so will not be down till tomorrow. Danced for an hour or two.

17 Saturday

Mr. Willis got the fever at about 1/2 past 9 this morning and has been raving all day. This evening he got better, and played for us girls to dance. He danced with me once, but no more, as he did not feel enough energy. We came into the sitting-room at about 9 & I sang to them from Mrs. Shadforth's new music. Mr. Tudor came this afternoon. He met a man on his way down who had had lunch with Harry & Mr. Bob at Gibson's crossing. So they got so far safely. They are here for the mustering.

18 Sunday

Mr. Lamond came back this morning, but did not come over until the evening. It has been a wretched day. The morning & afternoon were both disagreeably long. Mr. Willis & I quarrelled this morning & have not spoken since. Mr. Tudor, Edith & I went for a walk this afternoon to pick some wild flowers. Mr. Shadforth & Ernie were out on the Run all the afternoon.

19 Monday

Mrs. Shadforth's birthday, and great cooking has been going on. I was washing all the morning & ironing until late in the afternoon. The boys had some races round the race-course, which was a relief to the usual monotonous routine of the days. If Harry comes back this way I shall beg him to take me out. I am so tired of being without him. Mr. Tudor, Edith & I went for another walk to get flowers this afternoon. Mr. Johnson came down for the mustering here, this afternoon.

20 Tuesday

All the young fellows except Mr. Tudor, who had an accident & could not go, went out on the "Run" mustering. We had a nice quiet day, except for its being horribly long. In the evening Mr. Tudor, Edith & I went for a stroll, & in less than 10 minutes we saw two snakes, & killed one, the other got away. Mr. Doyle spent the evening here, to go out with Mr. Shadforth & Mr. Johnson on the Run the first thing tomorrow.

21 Wednesday

Mr. Shadforth, Mr. Johnson & Mr. Doyle went off early & Mr. Tudor spent the morning at home. He went to join the others & returned with them after luncheon. Mr. Tudor taught me to plat[33] cabbage tree hats this morning, so I shall make one as a curiosity to take down south.

22 Thursday

They all went off with the cattle to Mr. Doyle's yard to brand, & returned to luncheon, left directly after & did not return till sundown. I was rather low spirited all the evening. Ernie was going to take me to watch the cattle with him last night from 10 till 12, but Mr. Shadforth would not allow me to go much to my disgust, as there is a wild cow among the mob.

23 Friday

Mr. Willis & Mr. Tudor went away after luncheon. Mr. Willis & I did not say "Goodbye" to one another. We are still in a state of animosity towards each other. I am so glad he is gone.

25 Sunday

I have had a horribly bad eye since Friday afternoon, it is better today, but is still much swollen and weak. It has gone all through the house, I am about the last to have it. ~~Mr. Ernie told me of a wicked story Mr. Willis told him of me & Mr. Tudor. The hateful fellow. Ernie told him, he did not believe it I am glad to say, but if he tells the same to strangers they will not know it is false. Poor old Harry, I hope it won't get to his ears.~~[34]

31 Saturday

Since I last wrote I have been blind in one eye & half so in the other. Today I am better I am thankful to say. I pity anyone with the "Gulf Sandy Blight" it is perfect <u>agony</u>. Poor Ernie was bitten by a red spot

---

33 That is, plait.
34 Unlike most other examples of parts of entry being struck through, in this instance the striking through is not of each word but rather in the form of a large "X" in pencil.

black spider on Wednesday night & since then has been suffering frightfully. This morning & afternoon, he has been frantic with the pain. It bit him on the nape of the neck & it swelled down his shoulder, & both that & his head is dreadful. The first night he was bad nearly all night, & they had to sit up with him (I was too ill), the next day until lunch time he was better, but in the middle of the day & at night the pain came on as bad as ever for 3 or 4 hours. On Friday he had no attack until 5 in the evening, when it was more severe than ever until he went to sleep after 2 doses of laudanum[35] at 10. I & the girls took it in turns to sit & take his hand. He nearly wrenched them off at times. Today he has been very bad all day. Mrs. Shadforth put an Epicacuana poultice on the bite the first night which they say must have done him good as he is not as bad as others who were suffering in the same way.

---

35 Laudanum, tincture of opium.

1 Sunday

Mr. Clark the other Sub inspector[36] came back with his detachment yesterday & came to luncheon & dinner today. I don't care much for him what I have seen as yet. The girls, Mr. Shadforth and Mr. Taylor went for a ride in the afternoon. I sat by poor Ernie all day nearly. He is very ill. [Illegible] was here from the Norman last week & he says Mr. Favenc is not coming until the next boat, so poor old Harry will have to wait all this time doing nothing. The next boat is due on the 5th.

5 Thursday

Four weeks today Harry has been gone. Ernie has been suffering terribly. The 6 days (which it is supposed to last) were over yesterday evening, & I think he is better today. Edith & I have been going for walks at daylight the last few days, & it is so delightful. Mr. Bob has not come yet, so I have had no letter from Harry, he is a fortnight over his time. The mailman too is 5 weeks late. We seem quite buried not having had any news for 9 weeks. Mr. Lamond & the troopers went to "Rocklands" last Friday to look for Mr. Crawford who has been missing for 5 weeks!

6 Friday

~~Mr. Willis came yesterday on his way to the Norman, remained all night & left immediately after breakfast this morning. We neither said "How d'ye do" nor "Goodbye" to one another, never spoke a word.~~[37]

7 Saturday

Ernie was almost well today. Mr. Clark was over for tea.

8 Sunday

Ernie took me for a walk with him & the black boy Sam to the waterfall about 2 miles from here in the morning. We got home at 1 o'clock & found they had finished luncheon, so we had ours in the store. The mailman came while we were out. Mr. Clark brought my

---

36 That is, of the Native Police.
37 Here too the striking through was carried out in pencil.

letters in the afternoon. I had a number of them, & one from Harry to my surprise. Heard from Lilla, Minnie, Annie, Sam,[38] Aunt Helen,[39] Mother,[40] Father,[41] Polly, Willie.[42]

9 Monday

Ernie went away to the L tree to work for Mr. Doyle. Mr. Clark was over to tea again. There is another letter from Harry, Mr. Clark found this morning, but the horrible man has lost it somewhere.

10 Tuesday

Washing in the morning. Amy & I killed a small snake on our way up from the wash-house. Mr. Murray came on his way to the Norman. He has found Mr. Crawford's remains. He was killed by the blacks. Mr. Lamond has gone on to get hold of the wretches & give them their desserts. Mr. Bob not turned up yet, we cannot imagine what is detaining him. He leaves (Mr. Murray) tomorrow morning the first thing. Sent by Mr. Murray letters to Mother, Annie & Sam.

11 Wednesday

To my intense delight & astonishment who should ride up but dear old Harry to take me away to Port Darwin with the exploring party. After all my loneliness for me to be going after all. Hurrah! We leave tomorrow. Harry brought letters from Louie & papa.

12 Thursday

Harry & I said Goodbye to Lilydale at 1/2 past 3 P.M. & camped all night at the "L-tree" with Ernie. Mr. Doyle had gone home when we got there. Poor Ernie was very ill with fever & ague[43] all night. We

---

38 Samuel Robinson, Caroline's older brother by three years.
39 Harry's Aunt Helen, married to his Uncle James, at Garna Villa Garna back in Ireland.
40 Harry's mother back in Ireland. Caroline's own mother had died in 1877.
41 Harry's father back in Ireland. Caroline's own father is referred to as "Papa".
42 William Lamb, who was married to Caroline's eldest sister Lilla.
43 Fever with hot and cold flushes. A spider bite is a possible cause, though in this case it is quite unclear.

cantered nearly the whole of the 16 miles. Willie Taylor, Amy & Edith came a few miles with us. We called in to see how Mr. Clark was, he is very ill with low-fever.

13 Friday

Left "L tree" at 9 A.M. & arrived at "Gregory Downs" Station where Mr. Favenc & Mr. Crawford[44] (the young fellow who is coming with us) are waiting for Harry to return with me. It has been raining a little nearly all day. We arrived at 1/2 past 4 & found that Mr. Favenc & Crawford had pitched our tent for us; so I did not get wet waiting about. We have not seen any of the Watsons from the house, & did not go up, as it is very wet.

14 Saturday

It was too wet to make an early start from "Gregory Downs", but as it cleared at about 11 o'clock, we had dinner, & they got the horses & we started at 2, or 1/2 past. Seventeen horses in all, 9 packed & 4 loose, & the other 4 we (Mr. Favenc, Harry, Mr. Crawford & I) were riding. We left the track immediately after crossing the Gregory river (which is close to the camp of last night) N.N.W. Course[45] and came across an open plain, for about 6 miles, travelling very slowly (3 miles an hour) on account of Mr. Favenc's having to consult the compass every few minutes. There was no rain, but cloudy & threatening all day. We arrived at our camp for the night at about 10 min past 4, & immediately the packs were off the horses, Mr. Crawford went to the waterhole, & shot 3 ducks (which are cooking for tomorrow). Mr. Favenc & I made the fire & got tea ready, & Harry put up our tent, & got things straight for me. For tea we had salt beef, damper & potted meat. The rest had billy tea without milk, but I had chocolate et lait as I don't like tea without milk. Harry brought me that which I enjoy. It still looks very threatening. We are in our tents for the night & it is only 1/2 past 7.

---

44 Lindsay Crawford, the fourth member of the main expedition. Not to be confused with the Mr. Crawford whose fate had just been established.
45 "N.N.W. Course" was added in ink.

15 Sunday

It has been drizzling rain in showers all day, so we have remained in camp. It has seemed very little like Sunday. We got up at about ½ past 6, & Harry went to look up the horses, & we got breakfast. Mr. Crawford made a damper sweetened with raisins & currants which is a very good bushman's cake. Harry & I went to the waterhole, & he shot at some ducks, but did not kill any, but wounded two, which we were unable to get. In the afternoon they shod 3 horses after which Harry again rounded the horses. We are in our tents for the night, just going to bed at 7 o'clock, not quite dark. I did nothing all the afternoon but wash out a pair of socks. When travelling we all wear revolvers & the gentlemen have rifles slung on to their saddles.

16th Monday

Five minutes to 7 P.M. In our tents for the night. It has been fine but cloudy, only 2 or 3 slight showers. Rose at daylight, breakfasted at about 6 & left camp at 7. Crossed a good sized creek at once, on the way to which we saw a big carpet snake, but did not stop to kill it. Travelled through first a plain & then through 17 or 18 miles of thickly wooded plain country, with coarse grass about 4 or 5 ft. high. Picked and ate a quantity of native black currants, a small black fruit growing on high bushes. They are very sweet & not much taste. Rather sickening to eat too many. We passed a blacks' wet weather camp, which had seemingly been deserted 3 weeks or so. There were 4 humpies made of the coarse grass growing all around, bound roughly together with strips of bark. They are built in a semi circle, with no front part, all open. It is only during the rainy season they inhabit them, in fine weather they lie in the open country under trees. We got to camp after riding about 20 miles. We are on the banks of an almost dry creak, there are little bits of water here & there. After unpacking a pack horse & unsaddling mine, I washed out some of Harry's soiled clothes, which was hard work, as he got them so very dirty. All along the way today we saw signs of the Blacks, viz. holes in trees out of which they have got possums & sugar-bags. (native honey) Didn't stop for dinner, 7 hours in the saddle! N.W. course.

17th Tuesday

A long journey without stopping for dinner today. Mr. Crawford made me some sandwiches, & we each had one, so we were not quite so famished as yesterday when arriving in camp. We left at 9 A.M. & got to camp at a little past 4. On our way Mr. Crawford shot 2 fine black ducks, & I curried them this evening for tomorrow morning's breakfast. Mr. Crawford made a damper & cake. We are camped by the side of Lorne Creek, a beautiful large piece of water, lined with pandanus or corkscrew palms. N.W. course. The flies are frightful! Did about 25 miles.[46]

Wednesday 18th

Currie filled with flies, uneatable. We had the curry for breakfast this morning and I accused Mr. Crawford of leaving the quills in the ducks instead of plucking them clean. Later however when it was broad daylight when I went to empty the remains of the curry out of the billy I discovered the supposed quills to be thousands of flies which had evidently blown off the long grass as I was making it. The grass everywhere is simply covered with flies. The men after discovering that they had had a meal of flies were all ill.[47]

Got up at daylight, & left camp at 1/2 past 8. Got into camp again on a branch of the river Nicholson (supposed to be a very bad place for the Blacks) at 1/4 to 4. We sleep every night now with 2 revolvers in bed with us, & a double barrelled breech-loader. Outside, at the tent door a loaded carbine Schneider stands all ready for use. At about noon today we had a very boggy creek to cross & my horse got bogged and as it was trying to right itself, in going up the bank it fell on its side, & I came over on my back, but fortunately for the party, I was none the worse for my intimate acquaintance with the mud, but rather enjoyed it, as a relief from the monotony of the day's ride. At present, we have been travelling over very uninteresting country. We had several very tiresome gullies to cross, one they had to put branches across to prevent the horses bogging beyond remedy. Harry & Mr. Crawford carried me dandy chair

---

46 The last sentence was added in pencil.
47 This paragraph was added in pencil to the day's initial entry.

fashion[48] across this one. It was very warm all day, in spite of a nice cool breeze blowing. Steering a N.W. course again today. We had some sandwiches today for luncheon, so we were not quite so starved as usual when arriving in camp. Did some more of Harry's washing this evening. Came only about 17 miles today owing to the constant stoppages in the bogs. The flies all day have been very troublesome, and the mosquitoes too.

19th Thursday

The horses had wandered so far during the night, that Harry & Mr. Favenc were from daylight until 9 finding them, so we could not get away from camp till 10. We made up the hour however, by not camping for the night till 5. We had rather an unpleasant day's ride. Almost directly we left last night's camp, we crossed the Nicholson, one of the largest rivers (when full) in Australia. It had very little water in, but it had 5 or 6 arms all of which we crossed, & in the wet season it is one huge river. After crossing we came to a camp evidently used last night, as there were tracks of a large mob of cattle, & we came up with a mob soon after. We travelled for some miles along the Port Darwin road, but left it again at about 3. The track (for it was merely a track) was so very dusty & it was so very warm, that we were glad to leave it and go into the trackless bush once more. We saw two cattle camps on our way today, but didn't speak to the men. This evening after tea, while Harry & Mr. Crawford were counter lining my saddle (which has given my mare a bad back) a Mr. Richardson rode up to the camp, thinking we were one of the camps we passed; he had some tea, & is now just going on again! Mr. Favenc knew him before, but neither of the others did. We are camped in a nice place; but the water in the two holes we are at is so muddy that when the water boils in the billies, the dirt can be taken off by spoonfuls. The tea & cocoa when made is quite black. Not a sign of a Black all day, (so much for the Nicholson's being so infested with them). We are still close to the Nicholson, following it up for a little distance. We did about 19 miles today.

---

48 That is, Crawford and Harry both held their own wrist with one hand while clasping the free wrist of the other with their other hand, thus forming a square "seat" on which Caroline might be transported with a modicum of elegance.

Friday 20th

The horses were close this morning, so we made a start at 20 minutes past 8, and did a long stage of about 8 1/2 or 9 hours, but only travelled about 24 miles, as we stopped for 1/2 an hour or so getting some luncheon out of the pack bag at 1 o'clock. We arrived in camp at 5 o'clock on the bank of a creek with no name. Mr. Favenc asked me to name it, so I gave it Mr. Crawford's christian name "Lindsay". It was rather hot, but not nearly so many flies. We passed the borders of Queensland at 1/2 past 4 & are now in South Australia.[49] The country is by no means pretty or good in any way. The only redeeming feature is that there is plenty of water. The white ants build enormous nests in this part of the country, some we saw today were fully 9 ft high in the shape of a sugarloaf.

Saturday 21st

Left camp at 8 and arrived at camp tonight at about 1/2 past 4, after rather an exciting day. We went through a magnificent gauge[50] almost directly we started this morning. The rocks on either side of us were so immense, & a creak of lovely dark looking water by the side of where we were riding. We saw numbers of Blacks' tracks (footprints on the sand) evidently quite freshly made. All the way along, there were fires where the blacks were. Our way didn't take us close to any of them fortunately. Coming through the second gauge, we saw some fresh tracks of two blacks, gins & piccaninnies, & Mr. Favenc says a gin ran away from just beside him. He didn't see her, but he knows so well every little thing, that he must have heard something to come to that conclusion. We are in the really dangerous country now, & Mr. Crawford who has been staying in camp getting breakfast while Mr. Favenc & Harry went for the horses, says he will not stay any more, as the responsibility of having to take charge of me is too great, when Blacks are all around us; so Harry is going to take his place & stay in camp. There were some lovely

---

49 Twenty years earlier the Northern Territory had become part of South Australia. Despite considerable investment in infrastructure over nearly half a century the territory did not deliver the riches many South Australians had expected, with the result that the Commonwealth took over administration in 1911.
50 Gorge.

flowers on the road today. We stopped in the middle of the day for a half an hour for luncheon. Did about 20 miles.

Sunday 22

Left camp (without any attack from Blacks) at 1/2 past 8 this morning and had a longer day in our saddles than we have yet had, not arriving at a camp until after sun-down (1/4 to 6). We "spelled" 1/2 an hour or so for luncheon in the middle of the day, & rode all the rest of the time. We were so late in getting to camp on account of not being able to find water. Now, there is only one dirty little pool in the sandy gully we are at, & they had to dig a hole for our drinking water. We did not see a sign of Blacks today, except their fires in the distance, (or the smoke rather). It was very uninteresting country all the way, and as we saw no signs of Niggers, we feel pretty safe from any attack tonight. Last night, I was awake on & off nearly all night being nervous. Mr. Crawford took the lead all day & Mr. Favenc, Harry and I drove the pack horses. The poor animals have nearly all sore backs, it seems so cruel to be obliged to ride & pack them. Counting the hunting for water, we travelled about 25 miles in all. This has seemed very little like Sunday I am sorry to say. Rode all day with revolvers in our hands in case of an attack from Blacks.[51]

Monday 23rd

Left camp at 1/2 past 8 this morning after their having a good deal of trouble finding the horses, but we were up earlier than ever (the moon was still shining brightly). We have only come about 10 miles today, but we had a high stony steep mountain to come up, and the horses were tired so we came only 5 miles or so beyond it. We camped for 3 hours in the middle of the day for the horses to get a good feed and plenty of water, at the foot of the mountain, not knowing whether we should be able to get to water tonight on the "Table-land", & sure enough we have seen none since. Tonight for tea we were all on an allowance of a pannikin of water each for tea (we carried our 2 water bags full on purpose) (The bags hold 4 & 2 quarts, so until tomorrow sometime during the day, we have to make

---

51 This sentence was added in pencil.

that do.) We none of us ate any salt meat, or anything that would tend to give us a thirst. We are now on what is called the "Tableland", a flat piece of country on the top of a very high mountain. We are now in unexplored country where no white man has been before, so it is uncertain when we may see water again. We camped this evening at about 1/2 past 5. On our arrival at the Tableland Harry killed a carpet snake 7 ft long just beginning to climb a tree. No tracks of Blacks all day.

Tuesday 24th

We were until 2 o'clock this afternoon without getting to any water, nearly 24 hours the poor horses were without it, & I had nothing since tea time last night, as I knew the others could not enjoy breakfast without any tea, & I could. We are now camped by the side of a large, beautiful lagoon, which Mr. Favenc has named "The Caroline" (at Harry's suggestion) after me. He is giving all the rivers, etc. names for the South Australian Government. We saw tracks of Blacks today, but no very recent ones. We left camp this morning at 8 & travelled about 22 miles, arriving early in camp this afternoon, not having waited for luncheon in the middle of the day, there being no beef boiled & no damper baked on account of not having water last night. There was some lovely pink heather growing about the country today, but unfortunately we could not get a plant as to carry such a thing on pack horses would be impossible. Mr. Favenc marked a blue scented gum tree by the side of the "Caroline" with the name of the lagoon with a broad arrow over it. Saw tracks of Emus and native dogs (dingoes) but did not see either. The brand of the tree was

Wednesday 25th

We left the "Caroline" at a few minutes before 8, & arrived in camp by a nice little waterhole at about 5, having waited an hour in the middle of the day to boil the billy as we thought it possible we might not get water again for some time. We were agreeably surprised to find ourselves camped by it tonight. This is evidently a Blacks' camping place, but from the appearance of the old ashes from the fires & no foot tracks they cannot have been here very lately, but they say it is a standing camp as there are some stones about which they use for sharpening their stone knives, so they must intend returning, or they would have taken them away with them. We travelled all day through very scrubby country, no scenery worth anything, mostly plains with sandy soil & little scrubby bushes all over it, with tufts of "spinnifex" (grass) every here and there. Spinnifex is a grass which nothing eats, so this country is of no value. We are camped on a nice little patch of good grass, fortunately for the poor horses. Mr. Favenc marked trees today with a broad arrow, one at a creek we crossed, & one here on Tea trees. We saw several Blacks' fires on our way today at some distance away.

Friday 27th

(Writing just at sunrise by my pack saddle & bags waiting for Mr. Crawford to bring back some of the horses that have gone astray –) Yesterday morning "Trooper" wandered away in the night, consequently we made a late start not leaving camp till 9 o'clock. We did about 11 miles & at 12, we waited by the side of a waterhole while Mr. Favenc marked a tree, & then we went on about 2 miles further & got off our horses for a few minutes to eat a piece of bread & meat & damper cake. From the place the tree was marked we brought the 2 water bags full of water, & used them for luncheon, never suspecting we would find a difficulty in getting any more, or we might have stinted ourselves then, but so it was we travelled on until 11 at night & then had to camp without water. Just at dark we waited for a few minutes, while the lantern was prepared, & had a piece of cake, & opened a tin of stewed fruit to try in that way to partially quench our extreme thirst. It had been very hot and dusty all

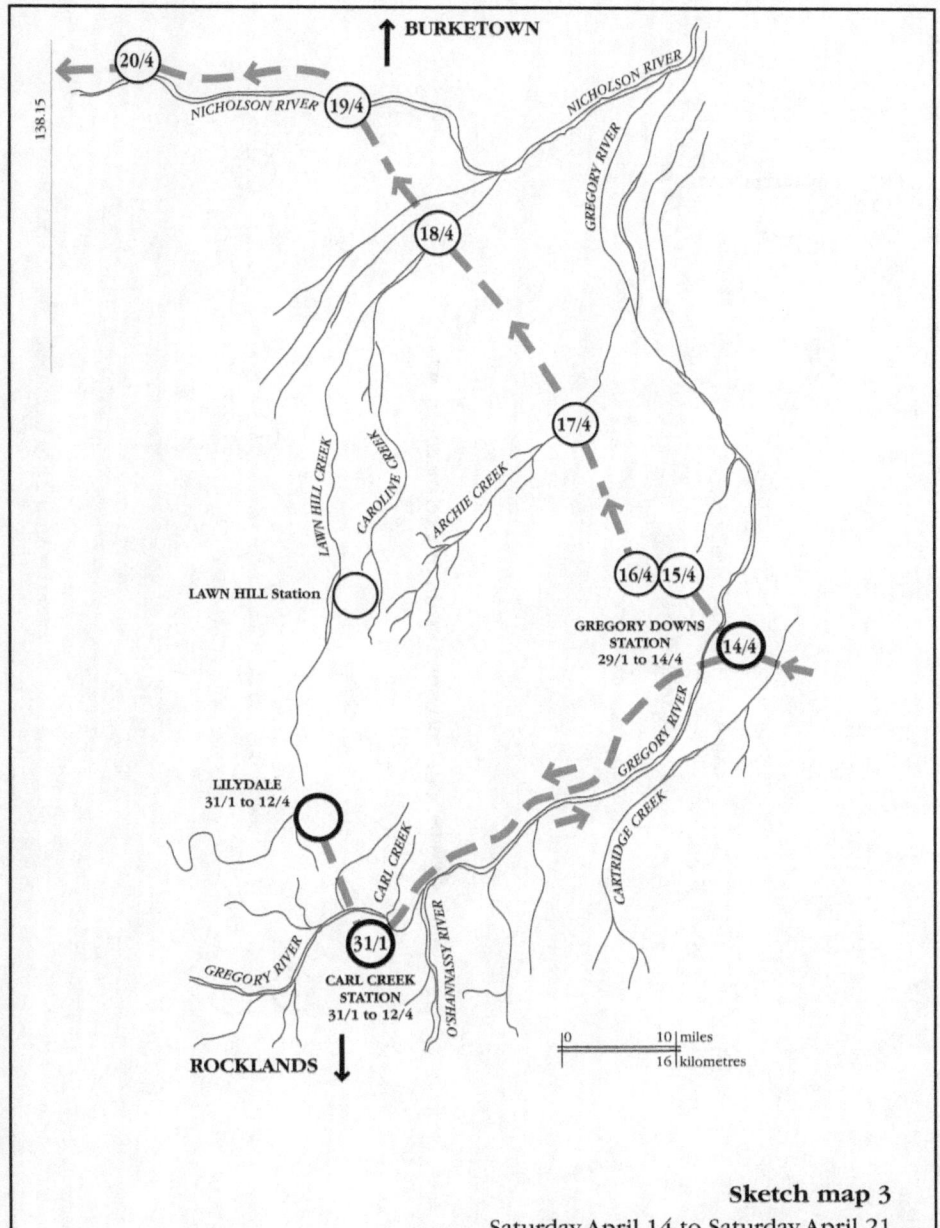

Sketch map 3
Saturday April 14 to Saturday April 21
Carl Creek Station, Gregory Downs Station then **exploring** up to
the state border South Australia/Queensland

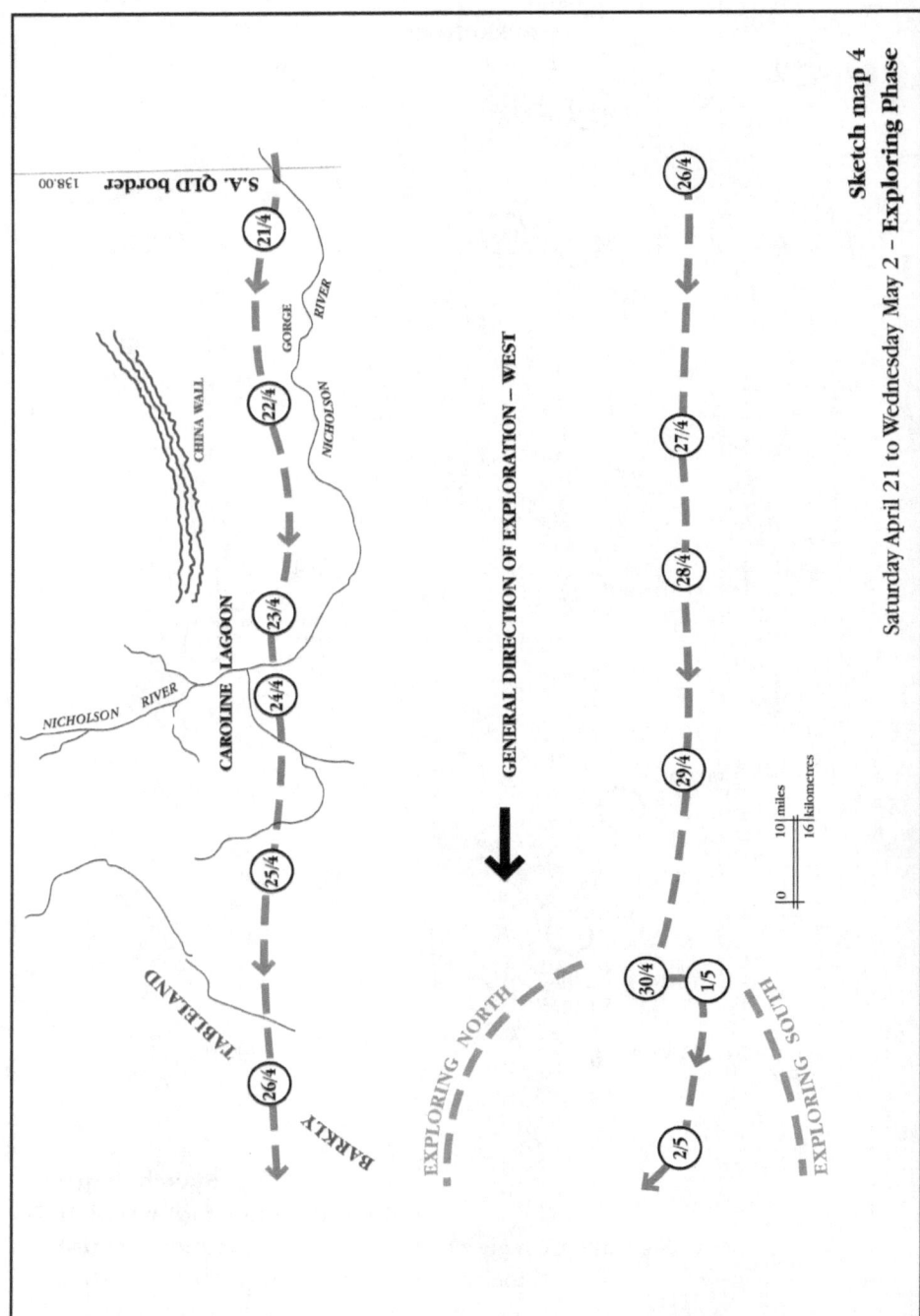

the afternoon, so by the time we opened the fruit we were parched. We wasted as little time as possible, and went on again, Mr. Favenc taking the lantern on ahead and we 3 driving the packhorses with considerable difficulty, as they were accustomed to being in camp 2 hours at least before then. If there had been grass anywhere we should have stopped, but there was none but "spinnifex", so on we were obliged to come. At first for 2 hours we had a good deal of difficulty getting along in the dark, what with thick scrub, & having to pay all our attention to the horses for fear of losing one in the dark. At 9 the moon rose, & although the stars had been shining brighter all the time it made a wonderful difference, & we got along much easier. Poor Harry & Mr. Crawford were nearly falling from their horses with sleep they got off and walked leading their horses occasionally to wake themselves up. In the middle of the night-journey one of the horses bucked and sent his pack flying. They managed to find everything with the aid of the lantern except Mr. Favenc's sleeping mat, and that we were obliged to leave. At 11 the horses & we were so tired & thirsty we could not go on, so we opened two more tins of preserved fruits, and drank the juice greedily. We then threw our blankets under trees too tired to put up tents, & went to sleep almost immediately. We travelled about 30 miles in all yesterday, & were 14 hours in our saddles, with the exception of those few minutes at 3 different times, which certainly eased us slightly, short time though it was. I am still very thirsty, & we are going on immediately to find water before we attempt breakfast. It is very cold at night now, & Harry & I find 2 blankets hardly enough to sleep comfortably. The days are still very warm. We saw two or three Blacks' fires, but none closer than 9 or 10 miles.

(Evening) We arrived at a water hole at about 11, much to our delight, & also to pretty good grass, so we camped for breakfast & dinner combined, & left again at about 4. Harry put up the flie of the tent for me to lie under and rest while Mr. Crawford made another waterbag, & Harry put a pad onto my saddle, as my mare's back is very sore. We passed during the morning several burnt pieces of country where the Blacks have lately been burning to catch animals.

The way they manage, is to light a big fire over a good space of country, and as the animals run out to escape being burnt, they catch & kill them. They lit one of these fires about 3 miles from us where we were camped, but we saw nothing of them. We left there at 4 & came on thinking we might not get water, so were supplied with sufficient to last until after breakfast tomorrow. However, when we got about 6 miles we came upon water & good grass, so we are camped for a few hours, & will proceed at about 1/2 past 3 in the morning if possible.

Saturday 28th

We did not wake till daylight, an unusual thing with any of us, but I suppose we were tired out. We left camp, (Uxine Creek we called it) at 9 & stopped at 12 for luncheon. We carried water with us & boiled the billy for some tea, left there at 1 & came on looking for water till 7. Got (to our surprise & delight) to a nice water hole. The country looks so dried & parched up that we expected to find none tonight. The poor horses were nearly mad with thirst, & we too having been on short allowance, were not sorry to get as much as we required. One of our horses has been very ill all day, it has tried to lie down several times, but we managed to get him to camp, but we expect to find him dead in the morning. Travelled about 25 miles through desert country, no grass, slightly timbered with gum trees principally. No birds or animals of any sort, except a dingo, which shewed us we were near water. Mr. Favenc marked a large tree with a broad arrow & underneath cut all our initials.

Sunday 29th

Poor old "Leichardt" did not die, but was much better this morning. We left camp at 9 and travelled through horribly rough & uninteresting country all scrubby and full of nasty holes. Stayed half an hour for luncheon at 1, & saw signs of water (viz. cattle tracks) & followed them up and came to a nice little water hole at about 1/2 past 6. The poor horses were just famishing for water. We had brought a supply to last for 2 or 3 days if necessary, so we were not so anxious for ourselves, but we would have been obliged to go with unwashed hands or face until we did get to it, so of course we were delighted, as by the time we get to camp at night, we are by no means <u>clean</u>! Travelled about 24 miles. Still going west. We are camped tonight on an open plain, with only trees round the water hole, which is a vast improvement upon our late, scrubby camps. We have christened this place "Broad's Park" as it is supposed to be on his country.

Monday 30th

Remained in camp all the morning with Mr. Crawford, while Mr. Favenc went to the North 10 or 12 miles & Harry to the South the same distance to explore Broad's country which we came on to yesterday. Harry returned at 2 having been away 5 hours, & Mr. Favenc an hour later. We immediately packed the horses and came on about 6 miles, and camped without water at just before dark. The horses drank at noon so they are not thirsty & we carried plenty for drinking purposes until tomorrow night. We shall not be able to wash at all which is very annoying, as we are all very grubby. We came through the same sort of country as yesterday only the grass was much better. Came by several old Blacks' fires.

Tuesday 1st

We got up by starlight this morning, & left camp at 1/2 past 7. Arrived at a good waterhole at 1/2 past 8. Since then we have seen no water & no appearance of any in our proper course, so as the horses must have some tomorrow, it is undecided whether we are to go back to the waterhole we were at this morning, & one go on with a pack horse, & carry water for horse & man to Powell's creak[52] 100 miles from here to send Mr. Broad the telegram about his country which he was to have had yesterday, the rest of us waiting in camp at the waterhole until his return when we would go & look for water – not being pressed for time. We came about 19 miles in our course & then came on 5 miles south following an empty creak, thinking we should come upon water, but it ran out completely so we are camped. Harry left us at the bed of the creak where we camped for luncheon to explore country 7 miles from there to the N.E. & did not return to this camp till 1/4 past 6 just before dusk. I was getting very nervous as we saw fires in the direction he was going, but as it turned out he did not come upon any Blacks, the fires were some few miles farther away. Mr. Favenc left us when we got to camp at 1/2 past 3, to look for water out west, but came back at about 8 not successful in his search. We had a large fire burning & a lantern hung up a tree to guide him back to the camp, as we are on a plain slightly timbered & bush all round, & as it is very dark, he would have had some difficulty in finding his way, as the grass is high & thick, & if one is a 1/4 of a mile from the camp the tent is hardly visible. We came over "plain" country all the way today. The flies still torment the very life out of us from sunrise to dark. The cold nights don't seem to kill them, they come back in millions in the day. No mosquitoes fortunately. The sun gets very hot from 8 in the morning & lasts hot till 5. I don't believe the days are ever cool in this country, however, it is not nearly such killing heat as we endured in January, February & March.

---

52 Powell Creek Telegraph Office on the Overland Telegraph Line.

Wednesday 2nd

Mr. Favenc and Mr. Crawford took the horses back to the waterhole we were at yesterday to get a drink, as they could not go on, as it was so probable we might be some time in finding it. They left at 1/2 past 6 & returned at 3, & we packed up immediately after they had had a hurried luncheon & started at 4. Harry & I remained in camp doing odd jobs all the morning. It was very hot today. We have had cloudless skies for nearly 3 weeks, & no appearance of rain, until it comes it will continue to be hot & the flies will go on tormenting us. We are reduced to damper & honey, as we have finished our cooked meat & no water to boil the one piece that remains. We have some anchovy paste, but are afraid to eat it on account of its tendency to create thirst. We finished our meat yesterday morning, so we shall not be sorry to get some more, as damper & honey are not very nourishing. We had some preserved potatoes tonight as they take very little water & it was a change. Mr. Favenc & Crawford took all the waterbags this morning leaving us the little that remained from what we brought yesterday, to have for breakfast & lunch. We came on until about 8 tonight, Mr. Favenc carrying the lantern as on the previous night. We have not come upon water, but the horses can do without it for some hours tomorrow, & we trust we shall come upon it soon. I had a tiny scrap of water spared me this morning to rinse my hands & face, but I feel extremely grubby. We came over very rough country this afternoon, we all had very narrow escapes from being thrown off our horses, for the holes were so numerous, & deep, that it was only by holding on tightly & being on our guard, that we managed to stop in our saddles when the horses stumbled into them. Fortunately the ground changed shortly after dusk so we had not darkness to contend with too.

Thursday 3rd

This has been a very eventful day. We left camp soon after 8 this morning anxious to hurry as much as possible to reach water early. We continued our right course (W.) for an hour, & seeing no signs of water, viz. emus' & native dogs' tracks, or flocks of birds, Favenc changed our course to the north. We went on passed a dry creak, till

2 & almost despairing of getting water when we saw not 3 miles straight ahead of us a Blacks' fire (or smoke rather) so we made for it knowing there must be water where niggers were. We reached the fire & were going round it, when Favenc made a gallop & Crawford followed from behind with us, & we knew they must have seen niggers. I wanted to go on too, but Harry wouldn't hear of it much to my disgust. However we went on with the horses after them, & presently we got up to them & saw Mr. Favenc holding a man with one hand & in the other pointing his revolver at him, & Crawford holding a gin. They were a peculiar sight. They had never seen white men before we soon found out, by their showing no fear when Favenc pulled out his revolver. When Mr. Favenc came upon them, they climbed up a small tree and when he made signs for them to come down the nigger threw his gin down thinking that might satisfy them, and it was some little time before he was induced to come down himself, when Favenc tied him with a strap to prevent his running away before he had led us to water.[53] We were not going to do them any harm we merely wanted them to take us to water, so they remained captives till we had shewn them, by giving them some water to drink out of our bag & signing what we wanted them to do. They then went on, with a great many gesticulations which we suppose meant fright, and after taking us about 3 miles, we came upon the camp & a waterhole. There were 7 men & 9 gins & some piccaninnies. The gins bolted at our appearance & we saw nothing of them. One poor little baby was left by the mother in her fright, & it was toddling about crying. The blacks wear no clothing of any sort. One man had a carpet snake which he had killed round his waist, ready to cook for his supper. The poor things were quiet & frightened. Not having been molested by white men, they did not attempt to do us any harm. When we went down to the water hole, they all took up their boomerangs, so Harry remained on the bank with his revolver ready to fire at the first throw. They soon put them down, & came & stood about 20 yards away while we had dinner. We gave them some damper & they seemed pleased. We left their camp at 4, & came on till 8, through a dreadful scrub. How we got through in the dark without accident I don't

---

53 The section beginning "When Mr. Favenc came upon them ..." was added in pencil.

know. We soon had the fire lit & the billy boiling for our meagre supper. We saw several spears and things lying on the ground in their camp, but they would not allow one to take anything away, as harm has been done so often by white men stealing the Blacks' only means of gaining their food. The man we caught first had a white plaited string made of bark round his head, & he threw it down when Favenc let him loose, a sign of submission & peace. All the men amongst these Blacks are circumcised.

Friday 4th

We were all very tired this morning so none of us woke till nearly sunrise, but as the horses had had very little to eat all yesterday, they were too hungry to go away from the camp but were feeding round our tents ringing their bells lustily all night long. We left camp at 1/2 past 8, made haste to get to water, but have been unsuccessful. The poor horses are looking rather pinched for want of water having been travelling all day in the heat. We camped for a few minutes in the middle of the day & ate our last pieces of cake & damper. We camped for the night without having come to water, & after having gone after various (as we thought) seeming watercourses, at 6 o'clock. No damper to eat, & no water to make any. We had enough to boil some rice, & a pannikin of tea each, & we have to be satisfied with that until we come to water. The rice we did not strain, because the rice water helped to quench our thirst. The horses being very thirsty, the 3 gentlemen are going to take it in turns to watch them. Mr. Favenc takes the first watch from now (8) to 11. Then Harry goes from 11 to 1/2 past 1, & Mr. Crawford from 1/2 past 1 till 1/2 past 3 when we begin to pack, so as to get water as soon as possible. We are sleeping without the tent tonight as it was late (8 o'clock) & Harry has to watch, so we are lying on our blankets with our clothes on. Travelled about 25 miles today in a very hot sun.

Saturday 5th

We (Harry & I) had very little sleep last night. Neither of us could sleep during Favenc's watch & when his turn came, I sat up all the time at first & then went one last time round the horses. We gave up watch to Crawford at 2 A.M. At 1/2 past 3 we got up & packed, but when we were ready to start at 1/4 past 4 there were some clouds which obscured the stars Favenc was going to take as his guide so we waited till 5 for the clouds to clear away. At first, for the half hour before daybreak, it was rather difficult to get the pack horses to follow Favenc, as the clouds were still rather thick over the sky, but after 6, we went on pretty quickly. The horses were already showing signs of knocking up, and at about 11 we thought we should be obliged to leave two of them behind, they were so weak & knocked up. However, after removing the packs from them to two of the loose horses that were not so bad, we managed to get them along slowly. As the afternoon advanced & no signs of water, the horses & we were feeling pretty well done. Fortunately the sun was clouded all the morning, or else certainly some of the horses would have succumbed. We had had nothing to eat since 7 last night, & only a mouthful of water each in the middle of the day, so finishing our last water, we had absolutely nothing we could eat. No rice, no damper, or meat. The only things we had were anchovy paste & some preserved milk, both of which would have increased our thirst. Harry & I had both of us to keep a smooth stone in our mouths to moisten our lips them in a small degree. We were getting almost hopeless, when the horses were getting worse & worse having been 50 hours without water, when Harry who had been again for the 5th or 6th time to see if timber ahead was a creak galopped back & told us if we held the horses, not allowing them to rush, there was enough water in a hole for us & them. How thankful we were to be sure. I immediately went on & I did have a good drink of muddy water. I enjoyed it however, as much as the clearest. I thought my poor little Gipsey would never stop drinking. She & all the horses were perfectly mad. It was no use trying to keep them. They smelt the water from a distance & several of them came headlong into the hole, & drank until they could scarcely move. The consequence of their rushing the hole, the clay at the bottom got all stirred up so that the horses that were kept back could get nothing but slush. Harry went on down the creak then to see if there were any more for the poor things, & after going about 2 miles he found a little more, so Favenc

& he took them all down, & they were satisfied. While they were away Crawford & I got a sumptuous supper ready consisting of some of everything in the camp. We boiled our last piece of beef, which I cut into small bits, to take less time cooking, as we were nearly famished, (not having tasted meat since Tuesday) cooked some rice & preserved potatoes, dried apples stewed, & a nice hot damper. We did enjoy our meal after having fasted 26 hours. We travelled South in search of water about 30 miles, being in the saddle 12 hours, with the exception of about 10 minutes at two different times, 5 minutes each time. I have had a nice wash, the first time since Sunday. I had not washed my <u>hands</u> for 3 days! We are all very tired & glad to get to our tents, having been awake nearly all night, & travelling since 5 this morning & nothing to eat or drink. The last 10 or 15 miles we came over a plain, nicely grassed, but rough for the horses; we are right in the middle of it tonight, with trees only on the sides of this creek.

Sunday 6th

We all had a good sleep this morning, not having breakfast till 8 o'clock. We left our last night's camp at about 1/2 past 10 to come to the other water hole as we finished the first one last night. We camped all day for the poor horses' sakes, they were so pulled to pieces yesterday. Mr. Favenc was out exploring all the afternoon, Crawford baking a damper & cake, & Harry not being well, slept until 1/2 past 5 & I lay down by him. When he got up we went & hobbled the horses, & had tea at about 7. We finished our last piece of beef this morning, so now we shall get no meat till we get to the Telegraph Station Powells Creak, which is only (Favenc imagines) 2 days journey if we went straight: he has exploring to do on the way so we don't quite know when we shall be there. It rained a little last night & the flies are if possible worse than ever. Harry & I had veils on in the tent all afternoon, & even those didn't stop them worrying.

Monday 7th

Left camp at 20 past 8 this morning, & came over the plain for about 13 miles, & found a nice water hole, with plenty of grass for the horses, so we camped at it at 1/2 past 1. Harry went away exploring after dinner, & Favenc went to shoot some birds if he could find any, as we were all hungering for meat. He brought some back & we enjoyed them thoroughly. I was patching my habit[54] all the afternoon under a large shady tree on the bank of the water hole. It would have been pleasant if the flies had not been so troublesome. I had my veil on all the time, but still they managed to get in somehow. It is almost impossible to remain 5 minutes during the day without a covering over the face. The poor horses have great holes under their eyes where the flies have been eating them. It has been cloudy all day, & tonight seems very much like more rain. Harry returned to the camp at a little before dark. He is still rather unwell, but better than he was yesterday. This camp is the nicest we have been in for a long time. ~~Favenc is making himself most objectionable. We might have known what to expect from a man who is not a gentleman~~ [... illegible][55] We had a narrow escape from the camp getting on fire when we arrived, the grass was so dry that a large patch was burnt before it could be stopped.

Tuesday 8th

Left camp at about 9. [portion crossed out – illegible] Poor old Harry is suffering from a severe attack of dysentery. When he went to look for the medicine last night, he found the bottle broken & all the contents gone, so he will have to leave nature to restore him. We stopped for lunch for a few minutes at about 2, then came on to a waterhole where we stopped at about 5. We stopped for about 3/4 of an hour at 12 at a waterhole to shoot some ducks which were on it. Crawford did the shooting but did not get any, but Harry shot 2 this morning while the others were out for the horses before breakfast, so we had stewed duck again for tea. All signs of rain have disappeared but there was a nice cool breeze blowing all day, so it was not uncomfortably hot coming across the open plain. There were a number of footmarks of Blacks all about the waterhole we are on, quite lately done.

---

54 That is, riding habit.
55 This section, the last part of which is illegible, was crossed out by Creaghe in ink. It is one of a number of signs of tensions within the party.

Wednesday 9th

Left camp at 1/2 past 8 & got into camp without water at about 1/2 past 5. We stopped for 2 hours or so at lunch time by a waterhole, waiting for Crawford who had been in a different direction looking at country. At 1/2 past 3 we stopped at a waterhole to fill all the waterbags as there was no signs of more water on ahead. We have been coming North all today. We are only 60 miles or so from the Powell, but have been thereabouts for 2 or 3 days. We are varying our course every day looking at Broad's country.[56] We saw numbers of Blacks' tracks in the different dry creaks we crossed, but no niggers appeared. The flat we are camped on tonight is full of immense holes, both Harry & Favenc have been up to their waists in two of them. We had some difficulty in getting a place free from one to pitch our tent. We saw no game today, so have been without meat again. Rice & dried apples (stewed), damper & honey constituted our tea tonight. Damper & honey & tea our luncheon.

Thursday 10th

This morning Favenc went away before breakfast to look for water, intending if it were close at hand to take the horses there and leave them all day while the 3 of them went in different directions with their riding horses only exploring. I of course would go with Harry. He had however a long distance to go & did not return to camp till after 10. We then packed & came to the water where we had dinner all together. After dinner (damper, potted ham & anchovy, preserved potatoes) Favenc & Crawford went away North exploring & will be away till tomorrow night. Harry decided to remain in camp with 13 of the horses, as we should be obliged to come back this way again & it was no use dragging the horses about when Favenc & Crawford could do all the work, so here are Harry & I alone in the bush. It is very desolate outside the tent, even the horses are away at some distance. There is not a sound of the bells, the only noise at

---

56 Andrew Broad and his partners, Alexander and Robert Amos, all from Sydney, had taken up huge areas of land in this region. Their station, "McArthur River", formed later that year, comprised more than 47 000 square kilometres. Favenc had been hired by Broad to explore their country. See Tony Roberts, *Frontier Justice: A History of the Gulf Country to 1900*, St. Lucia: University of Queensland Press, 2005, chapter 8.

present is some little insect or other, chirrupping. The weather is getting nice & cool now. The sun is hot but there is a cold wind blowing all day which is too cold in the shade, & which makes the heat from the sun very agreeable. There are several tracks of niggers all about this waterhole. It is to be hoped they won't attack us tonight. Harry has been very ill all day. I gave him some flour gruel & rice water, & hope they will do him good.

Friday 11th

In camp all day. We did not have breakfast till 1/2 past 7, rather too late for comfort the flies were all about. After our breakfast of preserved potatoes, & anchovy & damper, we went to round the horses up, & had to go a long way before we found them. I rode back on one of the quietest horses barebacked home & Harry walked beside me, as we had only taken one bridle out. We passed a Blacks' camp only a 1/4 of a mile from our camp. They had evidently been gone from it about a week. We went after the horses several times during the day, Harry was afraid of my being alone in the camp so I always went too. I washed all our soiled clothes & finished a woollen cap for Crawford. The 2 others returned just at dark about 7, when we were beginning to give up hopes of seeing them tonight. We had waited tea for them, not being in any great hurry as there was nothing tempting to eat, the old things, preserved potatoes, damper & anchovy. Harry has been slightly better today. I dosed him again with gruel made of flour, & he drank rice water, & I think they have done him good.

Saturday 12th

We did not leave camp today till 12 (noon) as Favenc expected not getting water till we get to the Powell which is 65 or 70 miles from our last camp (at least so Favenc thinks) & the horses would not take a good drink early in the morning. We came about 15 miles this afternoon, getting in to camp at 1/2 past 5. The reason for our stopping so soon was, there was no grass all the way along until we came to this, & there might be a long way to go before we get to any more if we left this patch, so we stopped. We passed no water at all, & have of course a "dry" camp tonight. The weather being so cool neither the horses nor we shall feel it so much as before. Harry is much better today. ~~Favenc is sulky & uncouth.~~

Sunday 13th

We had a terrible day from 6 in the morning till 11 at night. We left last night's camp at 8 A.M. & after about 2 hours riding got on to open "downs" country, ground full of small holes & very hard on the horses; not a tree to be seen at times anywhere round the horizon. A cold wind was blowing all day. We stopped at 1 for lunch in the middle of the plain. Crawford chased a turkey but did not succeed in getting a shot at it, to our disgust; not having had meat except at one meal since this day fortnight we were longing for some game. We followed one dry creek some little distance hoping to find enough water to give the poor horses a drink, but were unsuccessful. The poor things rushed madly along the creek looking for it, & it was with some difficulty we got them out at last. We had been 2 miles out of our course in this search, so by the time we had got back the 2 miles we had lost about an hour & a quarter, which we could ill afford not expecting to get any water till we arrived at the Powell. We travelled on until about 1/2 past 7, & then got into worse country for the horses than ever. The earth was just like deep soft sand with great pitfalls all over it. It was miserably cold & we were nearly famished, having had no meat for so long the 11 hours without food made us quite faint. The horses were getting knocked up with the want of water, hard travelling & so much work, we had great difficulty in getting them along the terrible country in the moonlight & to make matters worse we saw no grass for the horses. At last at 1/2 past 10 we got to a place where some herbs were growing but no grass to speak of, so we camped not knowing how much further we might have to go before we got anything better. I was off my poor mare in a second & lit a fire as quickly as I could with my numbed fingers. The billy was soon boiling, & we had a feed of damper & anchovy, we could not spare water for potatoes. We did not put up the tents, but just lay down in our clothes under a tree & needed no rocking to send us off to sleep immediately. It was so delightful to get between the blankets after the long cold riding. This morning before we got on to the plain we got some native oranges, they were over ripe unfortunately, so they had no taste in them. They were about the size of a small cultivated orange, & when ripe are green.

Monday 14th

Got up at streak of day & had a small breakfast of damper & a pannikin of tea each, finishing our last morsel of food until we get to the Powell which was about 30 miles as far as Favenc could guess. When the horses were brought up, a more miserable lot of unfortunate animals could hardly be found. Hector (the one that was so nearly done at our last long dry stage [)] lay down at the camp, & we were afraid we should not be able to get him through, & sure enough after 3 or 4 hours of very rough & sandy country, he knocked up completely. Harry & Crawford managed to whip him along for about 1/2 a mile, then the poor thing was done. No water being anywhere handy, Crawford shot him to put him out of his suffering. It was so horrible to have to leave him & three more we thought every minute would go too. However, at about 12, we got on to hard ground, scrubby, but good for the horses' tired feet & we got along better. At 4 we came to a creek (dry) which puzzled Favenc, he having been to the Powell before by a different route, & did not recognise it. We thought then we might possibly be still a good distance from the station, in which case some if not all our horses must go, & we might have to go hungry & thirsty too until tomorrow. At last we got to a range which Favenc knew, but did not know how far we were out of our course from the Powell, as the range stretched for miles opposite. We got on top of the range at sundown, & then we had a terrible piece of work; the range from the top extends some distance before it descends again, & the whole top of it consists of successions of frightfully rocky gauges, which we had to go up & down the best way we could. If it had not been moonlight we should have been done, as we could not have travelled over them, & most of the horses would not have had strength in the morning. As it was, we got on very well, & at 1/2 past 7, to our delight we came on to the telegraph line all of a sudden. Our joy was unbounded. The horses seemed to get fresh energy at sight of a beaten track (it is the road to Port Darwin too) & went on briskly. We did scarcely anything but talk of getting some substantial food to eat. We were literally starving. After going a mile or so, we got to wooden telegraph posts, & knew then we were only 5 miles from the station, as there are iron posts until within that distance on either side. The iron ones are standing because the Blacks cut them down if not watched. This line is the one communicating with the old country & there are telegraph stations about 150 miles apart from Port Darwin here to keep the line in order. When we got to five miles from Powell's Creek, Mr Favenc thought it advisable for one of them to go on to let them know there was a woman in the party, as no woman had ever been there before. So Mr Crawford went on & told them, but they wouldn't believe it until they saw me.[57] When we got to a dry creek on our way, the horses for some time were quite unmanageable. They rushed about madly in the creek for water, but after some little time finding none they became quieter, & we managed to get them on to the track again. When we actually did get to within 1/2 a mile of the water, they all (except 3 or 4 that were too weak) made one bolt, & did not stop till they found water. I thought the poor things would never stop drinking. We soon were up at the house and off our horses. There are 2 gentlemen in charge, a Mr. Bole[58] & Mr. Goss the assistant. They were both most hospitable & kind. We did not arrive till 10, & they got us a fine supper ready as soon as possible when they found we had had nothing since 6 in the morning. We enjoyed our supper of cold shoulder of mutton, sardines, salmon, good yeast bread & jam, & tea with milk in it out of china cups. They are out of sugar but that was nothing, no sugar in our tea was a very minor matter. The 2 gentlemen gave their room up to us, & they slept on the floor with Favenc & Crawford in the sitting room. This house is a good one made strongly, with high walls & no windows, as a protection from the Blacks. There are 3 rooms (a good size) in this building but there are good out houses which I have not seen yet. They were delighted to see us. I am the first woman ever been here, & we

---

57 The section from "When we got to the five miles . . ." was added in pencil.
58 The name is later corrected to "Bowley".

are the only strange faces they have seen here for more than a year, except the inspector of the line, who was here some 3 or 4 months ago. It looks so strange to see a house in the middle of the bush like this. We enjoyed our supper immensely, & were glad to get into a bed once more at about 12 o'clock. There are 3 or 4 men about the place besides 2 or 3 niggers half (civilised). There is a man cook & a labourer or two. Crawford used to be the Telegraph Master here about 2 years ago, so he feels quite in his element up here. The way they manage about rations is, the Government send up supplies once a year, & a certain number of sheep and cattle. They kill a sheep in summer every day I don't know how they manage in winter. I forgot to say that at about 2 o'clock we stopped for a few minutes & had some sugar to eat & a pannikin of water each, having nothing else to eat & all of us being hungry. We finished the water there too. We have done 80 miles in all without water, & took 59 hours over it.

Tuesday 15th

The telegraph has to be opened at 8 A.M. so we were up at a very decent time, & had breakfast at 8. after a delightful night's rest. All the morning I did nothing particular, lying down & reading principally. The 2 officers here make a great deal of us & especially of me, a lady is such a novelty to them. There are a small mob of Blacks camped close to the station. They are not civilised, but as long as there are several men about the place there is no fear of any danger. They are terrified at the sight of firearms, so many of them having been killed at different times. The S.A. government is very strict about murdering niggers, a man is liable to be hung for it, if it is found out, so unless the blacks have killed cattle or sheep the white men do not harm them, & then they have to keep it very quiet in case it should get to head quarters. The niggers have only seen me from a distance & they are most anxious to get a close view of a white "lubra" as they call a woman in their language. They have no clothes on of course, & are made to stay the other side of the creek at night in case of accidents. Mr. Crawford & Mr. Goss took the horses away to some good grass about 9 miles from here, the poor things are looking very woe begone. We had dinner at 12, & tea at 5. We

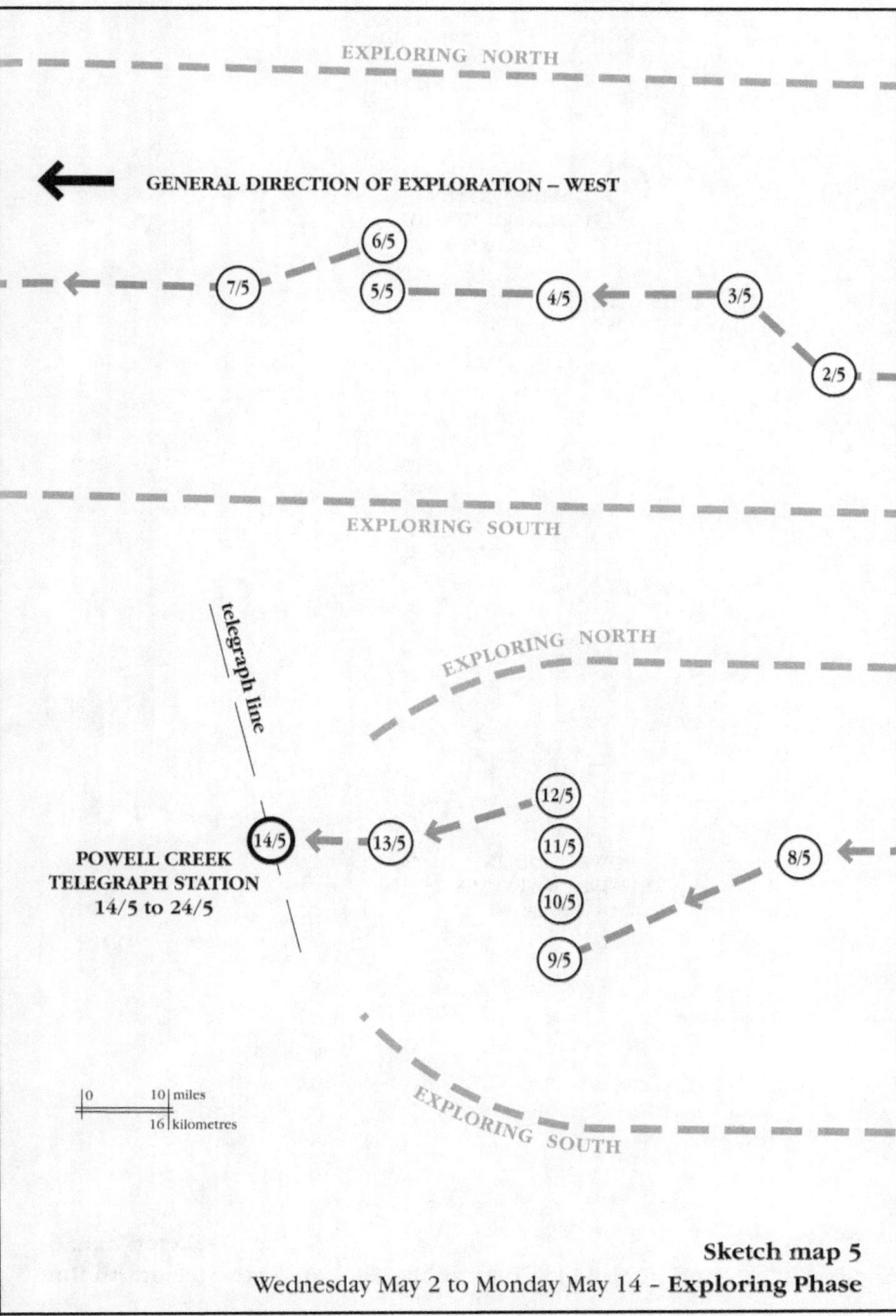

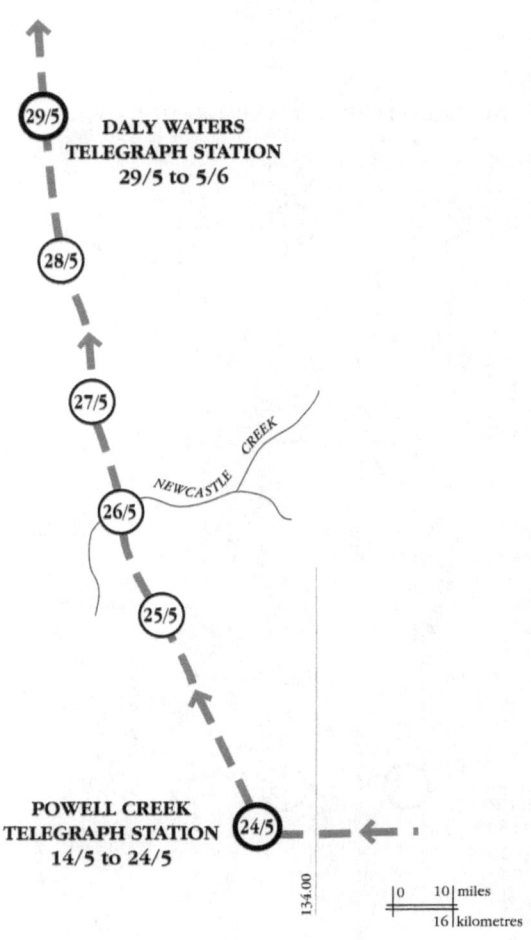

Sketch map 6
Monday May 14 to Tuesday May 29 - **along the telegraph line**

are all feeling decidedly better after our 4 good meals. In the afternoon Mr. Goss & I amused ourselves talking & looking over the buildings, & looking at the telegraph aparatus. In the evening Harry & I went for a short stroll, & then we came in & found the fire lit, & we all sat round & spent a very pleasant evening. We came to bed at about 10, after an enjoyable day of rest. Harry sent a telegram to Papa this morning telling him of our safe arrival. This evening Crawford was having a chat by telegraph to Mr. Murray the Station Master at the "Katherine" some 3 or 400 miles on the way to Port Darwin, & he & several others at the different stations on the line wanted to know if it was really true that a <u>lady</u> was at the Powell. Mrs. Murray, the only woman on any of the stations sent word to us that she intended to keep me when I got to their station. They are about 240 miles this side of Port Darwin, & she is considered a great wonder. The niggers had an idea there was no such thing as a woman among white people, they thought we were all men, so no wonder they were astonished at seeing a white "lubra".

Wednesday 16th

In the morning Harry got the water & washing tub ready for me down at the well the place the black boy washes all the clothes, & I washed & boiled all our things. I was busy there till dinner time. Harry & Mr. Bowley went out to try & get some turkeys for tea, but they came back at 11 without having had a shot at one. They have some splendid water-melons here, & they are a great treat, after having had no fruit for so long. There is a very nice vegetable garden, but the season for vegetables is only just commencing up in this part of the world, the summer being too hot, so we have had none. There is a peculiar thing up here which I have never heard of before & that is the water supply. This station is full of the native springs, & there are 3 or 4 wells entirely supplied by these springs. The earth is perfectly dry & it is astonishing where the beautiful clear water comes from. ~~Favenc continues to make himself unpleasant, he is very grumpy to us all except Crawford.~~ Did nothing particular all the afternoon & evening. Talked over the fire when it got chilly.

Thursday 17th

This morning after having well boiled our ration bags which were in a state of "filth", Harry took me to see the niggers, a number more of whom had come in early this morning I suppose & were camped a few hundred yards from the house in the bush. As we approached, the gins & piccaninnies bolted into the bush, but the [men] remained (8 of them) & after making signs & saying "Lubra" we got them to call the gins back. Only 3 of them came & would not bring their children. I suppose they were afraid we should steal one. They made us understand mostly by signs the 3 men to whom the gins belonged & they stood where they were, but the others turned their backs as the gins came up & did not look at them. I suppose unmarried black men are not allowed to speak to or take any notice of gins, until they themselves get one. The gins when married are not allowed to speak, they say everything by signs. The men & gins too are very fine looking as far as height & build go, but none but one of the ones we saw today were good looking. All the afternoon Harry was sleeping & I was lying down reading. After tea Harry & I went for a walk & then 4 of us went to the blacks' camp again & saw 5 of them corroborying. The rest had gone away somewhere. We heard afterwards that they had gone because they thought I was a devil devil"[59]

Friday 18th

Favenc, Crawford & Mr. Goss went up some creek close by here out of curiosity to see where it runs into, using the station horses. They will be away till tomorrow evening probably. This morning we were all busy at different things, this afternoon we all read & slept, & this evening after Harry's & my usual walk, we 3 spent a pleasant evening. ~~It has been a decided relief to have Favenc away, he never appears to get over his sulks.~~ Harry went down to the wash-house in the afternoon & washed his trousers!! The Blacks went away before we were up into the Bush again, so there are no wild ones anywhere close just now.

---

59 The last sentence was added in pencil.

Saturday 19th

We have done nothing particular all day. This afternoon at about 3. the 3 gentlemen came back. Harry & I went for two strolls in the afternoon & evening, but saw nothing wonderful.

Sunday 20th

This has seemed more like a "Sunday" than I have experienced for some time. Although all the men here do not value this day more than any other, they of necessity make a difference, as the telegraph instrument is closed except at certain hours during the day. Harry & I remained in our room till dinner & then until nearly tea time reading, so it seemed like Sunday to us. Crawford & Mr. Bowley went to see that the horses were all right & did not return to dinner nor till nearly tea-time, so Favenc not being a very amusing or entertaining companion Mr. Goss read to himself, so the house was nice & quiet. Harry & I went for our usual evening stroll which is about the pleasantest time in the day. ~~Thanks to Favenc & through him, Crawford is getting disagreeable also. We do not look forward to going out again with these two at all. Two pleasant men would make such a difference.~~[60]

Monday 21st

Our plans were all altered by Harry & Favenc last night. A great number of our horses are knocked up & if we were to take them on to the McArthur exploring as we intended, we should probably lose them, as it has been a very dry season, & consequently great scarcity of water will be on the way to the river, & in the horses' weak state they would perish. It is decided therefore that Favenc & Crawford should go out with 7 of the strongest horses, & we should go on with the remaining 9 to the "Katherine" 320 miles from here, & 250 from Port Darwin; & there wait until the other 2 return when we shall all proceed to Port Darwin, with fat horses instead of knocked up ones or still worse only half our number. Mr. Goss has got a notice that he is to go & exchange places with the assistant at the "Katherine"

---

60 The initial diary reveals the strained mood of the party by this time; the striking through here – as elsewhere – illustrates Creaghe's preference for discretion.

(which he only received this afternoon) so we shall travel down together which will be very pleasant. A waggon is going from here to the "Daly"[61] a telegraph station about 140 miles from here & as we shall have a long stage of 80 miles without water it is taking 2 tanks of water, so, to benefit by this water, we shall go with it as far as there. There is a good track following the telegraph line all the way, so it will be easy travelling compared with what we have been through.

Tuesday 22nd

Have been making preparations for our start tomorrow the first thing. Crawford & Mr. Bowley have been out all the afternoon & have brought all the horses but one, so unless Favenc who is going out again at daylight manages to find him early, we shall not be able to start until the next day, as we have 34 miles to go before we get to water.

Wednesday 23rd

We did not start today, for Favenc & Crawford went out before breakfast & were away until after dinner, & returned without having found the horse. "Billy" the black boy went out after they came back but did not return with the horses till nearly tea time, too late to start. The 2 men went on this morning, so we shall do long stages in order to catch up to them in 3 days.

Thursday 24th

Left Powell's Creek at 10 min past 9 this morning, & travelled along the road 35 miles not árriving in camp until 1/4 to 6. We are camped on the bank of a good sized waterhole. Favenc is taking 9 of the best horses out to the MacArthur & we have 5 only having sold 2 of ours at Powells Creek. It is very pleasant camping with an agreeable companion instead of what we have been going through. We saw no track of Blacks, although there are numbers seen on the way down usually. The river we are camped on is the "Newcastle", which is dry except in holes every few miles apart.

---

61 Daly Waters.

Friday 25th

The poor horses not having recovered from our recent hardships are getting knocked up already, so we only came about 16 miles today. We left camp at 1/2 past 9 & arrived at camp (still on the Newcastle on the banks of a jolly waterhole, with nice green grass down to the edge of the hole,) at 1/4 to 4. There is a splendid, large, shady gum tree which we rested & had our meals under.

Saturday 26th

Left camp at 1/2 past 9, & travelled 16 miles getting into camp on the end of the Newcastle (a splendid big hole) at 1/2 past 1. The dray from Daly Waters Station is here waiting to go with us, as there is no water between here & there a distance of 80 miles, so it has 3 tanks, so the horses can have water every night. There are 8 of us here tonight. The 2 men from Powells Creek who came on before us, & Mr. March one of the operators from the Daly & the 2 men driving the dray. We all go on tomorrow, the 2 men from Powells Creek returning there, & we 6 going on. We all, common men & all, had tea together which is not nearly such a cosy party as when we 3 are alone. The men from the Daly had some new papers (2 months old) which were a great treat to Harry, Mr. Goss and me. I haven't been feeling well today.[62]

Sunday 27th

Got up at 5 & had breakfast before daylight. Dawn does not break till 6 now. The 2 Powell Creek men went back & the dray went on at about 8, it took some time to catch & harness all the 6 horses. Our 5 had wandered some distance, so we did not make a start till 9. We caught up to the dray at about 11, & got into camp at 2, having come 20 miles. The first 5 miles we travelled through scrubby country, but the last 15 was across a bare plain. It was very hot & tiresome, & we were glad to get to the end, & camped on the edge, at the first trees

---

62 This is a first indication that Creaghe was pregnant. She might well have thought as much, though she never says so explicitly in the diary. She had been pregnant once before, probably with twins, but birth records suggest one was still-born, while the other, Cayley, died very young.

we came to. The dray arrived at 5, & we were glad enough to see it as it had all our things on board, so we had nothing to do but lie down & wait.

Monday 28th

We did not have breakfast until just before sunrise this morning, but as the horses were close we got away by 8 o'clock. We came about 16 miles & camped for lunch at 12. We waited for the dray, & got some of our things & some rations off it & came on another 9 miles to a tank which the dray had filled with water some little time ago, from the waterhole about 21 miles from here. The dray came on 2 miles from our dinner camp & stopped, as they have enough water in their tanks for their own horses. We got into camp at 1/4 to 6. If water is left in this tank, the Blacks often come & appropriate it, so until we came & found it nearly full, we thought they might have been before us, & then we should have been in a fix. It was hot today, only being off our horses from 12 till 1/2 past 2 waiting for the dray, we did not feel it so much, & besides we were travelling amongst trees, instead of over bare plains as we were yesterday. We did not bring on our tent this afternoon, as Mr. Goss is riding one of our horses, & as the only pack horse we have (except "Gipsy" – my mare – who has a sore back) is not very bright, we did not want to make the pack too heavy. We are sleeping underneath a tree tonight. I have been feeling squeamish again.[63]

Tuesday 29th

We left camp this morning at 20 minutes to 9, & stopped at 12 (having done 12 miles) for lunch. We waited until 3. as the sun was so hot, & as we had only 9 more miles to do to get to a waterhole, there was plenty of time to get into camp by sundown. Last night Harry and I both dreamt of Blacks. He dreamed that we were attacked by niggers & that both his revolver & mine full of cartridges missed fire. I dreamt that Harry had gone out & left me behind & that not having me with him, he neglected to put up the tent, & consequently he was knocked on the head & killed by the wretches – When we got

---

63 A further indication of her pregnancy.

into camp we saw numbers of fresh tracks of niggers, but did not think there was any danger of their being camped close by, as we were just on the road. I suppose Harry's dream put it into his head to fire off all his cartridges, & I did the same, so as to put fresh ones in, incase of accidents such as he dreamed of. It was fortunate he did so, for no sooner had we finished & begun to see about tea, than we heard a noise & looking up we saw, across the waterhole, some distance away among the trees 2 niggers. They threw up their hands in sign of peace, & Harry & Mr. Goss thought as it was not quite sundown, they had better allow them to come the camp, & see what sort of fellows they were, & send them off again before dark. No sooner did we beckon to the 2 to come, than 6 more appeared out of the bush with spears raised above their heads. After signing to them to put their weapons down they eventually threw them down in front of them, but Harry could see that they picked up the spears between their toes & were carrying them through the long grass that way. After more signs from him to leave them behind, they eventually did so.[64] When they came up we found they had seen white men, & one or two of them could speak a few words of English. After talking to them for a few minutes, Harry made them to understand we were going to camp there for the night, & they were to go away & come again at sunrise tomorrow, & they would get some food. The words used were "You know sun" (pointing to where the sun had just gone down,) they nodded their heads, "well, when sun come up" (pointing to the east) you come along, plenty "parter",[65] (hitting himself on his stomach). They understood & after waving their hands as goodbye they went off, but did not appear to go away straight, they lingered about the bush a good deal. As soon as they were gone, Harry said "We will saddle up & go on at once to the Station" (which was 14 miles further on). So we immediately packed up, & caught the horses & without waiting for tea made as great haste as possible to put some miles between us & the niggers. They were a horrid lot of looking men, & Harry would not trust them not to come back in the night. We should have had to watch all night, & there was no use

---

64 The section from "with spears raised above . . ." was added in ink.
65 Obviously means "food" but origins unknown.

in remaining in the middle of such danger when only 14 miles would bring us to the station. There must have been a large mob of blacks somewhere close, as these blacks said they had no gins, but that was a falsehood, as there never is a camp, but what there are several of them, so all things considered, the risk was too great, especially as there were only 3 of us in the camp, & neither Mr. Goss nor I are good shots. Two of the niggers were painted red, about the face & chest. The red stuff they get from a stone, they pick up among the hills. The way the niggers keep themselves warm at night without any clothing is they make two fires & sleep between them. They make their gins hunt for food for them, & if the poor unfortunate things return to the camp, without plenty, they beat & knock them about in a most fearful manner. We left all the damper & meat we had left in the camp, so that they would get it when they came up, were it in the night or the morning, as we had told them, they should have it. We came on at a good pace, & arrived at this Station Daly Waters, at about 10. This house is not nearly so good a building as Powell Creek. It is only made of slabs, & daylight is visible through every one. However, as the 2 in charge were expecting us shortly, they had prepared things to make me as comfortable as possible. We did 35 miles in all today, but I was not very tired, as the rest in the middle of the day freshened me up, & the last 14 miles was done at night. When we arrived, the cook (a Malay) had gone to bed, so we would not allow him to be waked up to get us a hot supper, so we just had some bread & preserved ginger, & then were glad enough to get into a bed again. Mr. Johns is the Station Master & Mr. Kemp the assistant. They are neither of them boys, & seem very quiet as yet. Mr. Johns has not seen a woman for 3 years, so no wonder he feels a little awkward at first. We shall probably remain here 6 or 7 days, as our horses need rest. The niggers were very much taken with the "white lubra", they scarcely took their eyes off me, nodding & smiling at me every time I looked up. I was feeling unwell all day again.

Wednesday 30th

Not feeling very well I was lying down all the morning and most of the afternoon. After tea I went round the place with Mr. Johns, & then Mr. Goss & I went round, & saw 2 graves of men who were speared by the niggers some few years ago. There is an iron bark tree about 100 yds from the house which Stuart the explorer of '69 marked with a large S.[66] It is going to be fenced in shortly. This is a very tumbled down, rambling place, but it will be replaced by a better one before long.

Thursday 31st

The dray came at dinner time. Mr. Johns asked Mr. Goss to remain here for 3 or 4 months & let him go down to the "Katherine" in his place, after which time, he is going south, & Mr. Goss can go on to his place at the "Katherine". Mr. Goss was goodnatured enough to assent but has been very low spirited at the prospect of remaining in this dull place for so long when he had expected to go at once to a Station where there is a lady & a piano & a rowing boat, & a mail once a week. Mr. Johns is beside himself with delight. I did some washing this morning, as I felt better.

---

66 John McDouall Stuart was there in 1862, either on his way to or from the Indian Ocean. He died in London in 1866. It was in 1883, the year of Creaghe's expedition, that a tree marked with the letters JMDS was located, confirming that he and his party had indeed successfully completed the crossing of the continent from south to north. See the *Australian Dictionary of Biography*, Vol. 6, Melbourne: Melbourne University Press, 1976, pp. 214–15.

Saturday 2nd

I was very unwell yesterday & am still today with dysentery. Today I have kept to my bed, feeling too ill to go out. Now is the time I miss little every day delicacies one gets in civilization such as milk, butter, eggs etc; when one is well, it matters not having to live on meat & bread (the latter made with flour almost too offensive to eat) & milkless tea, but one, when one's appetite is bad it is almost impossible to get such food down. I have been living today on dry toast & condensed milk to drink (we happened to have 1 tin left, there is none on the station). Yesterday evening just as we were sitting down to tea a Mr. McFee & a Mr. Jones with a man & 2 black boys came. The former on his way out to meet some cattle coming from Normanton & the latter going to take Mr. Goss's place at the Powell. They will be going away in a day or two I suppose. They were expected of course having had wires from the Katherine.

Sunday 3rd

I remained in bed until 2 or 3 this afternoon feeling very unwell. I got up and sat in a canvass chair then, but did not go out of my room. Mr. McFee & Jones went away after dinner.

Monday 4th

We are going to make a start tomorrow as I have been so much better today. Harry did our washing this morning, he would not hear of my touching the clothes after my recent indisposition. Mr. Kemp is coming down to bring up some cattle which are down at the "Elsie"[67] a "wet" telegraph Station between here & the "Katherine". As he is coming so far he will come on with us to the Katherine for a few days.

Tuesday 5th

We left Daly Waters at 1/2 past 9, 7 of us in the party viz. Mr. Johns, Mr. Kemp, Harry & myself, 2 men who have just finished some

---

67 A mis-spelling of the name of the Elsey Telegraph Station. The Elsey River had been discovered by Augustus Gregory on his expedition from the Victoria River to Brisbane and named after the expedition's doctor.

fencing work at the station, & are now going back North & their black boy. We camped about an hour & a half for dinner at 1 o'clock & then came on 14 miles further to a small waterhole, having done 27 miles in all. We did not get into camp till sundown. I haven't been at all well all day.

Wednesday 6th

Left camp at 8 o'clock & came on without any stoppages for 26 miles to a waterhole on which we are camped. We got in about 1/4 past 2, & after dinner I was busy till tea time making a damper cake, which we baked in the ashes, & a curry of salt mutton. The cake was a success (my first attempt at damper making) but the curry was too salt to be nice. I have been better today, but still slightly squeamish.

Thursday 7th

One of the horses got away this morning so we did not leave camp till 9. We did not stop until we got to this well 20 miles from last night's camp. We got here at about 1/4 to 2. This well was made when the telegraph line was being put up. It is 70 ft. deep, but there is very little water in it.

Friday 8th

Left camp at 8 & arrived at the "Elsie" at about 2, a distance of 26 miles. The pack horses with the 2 men came on in front today, so by the time we had had a wash, there was a nice dinner ready for us in the kitchen. This being only a wet season telegraph station, there is only one operator & the working men, & the office is his bedroom too, so we have our tent pitched close to the house. It is only a shed of a building, made of logs some 2 inches apart. It is nice & clean however, so it is quite pleasant in this hot climate. Here is the middle of June & the days after 8 o'clock until sundown are uncomfortably hot. There is a cattle station 4 miles from here, so we are gradually getting into civilization.

Saturday 9th

We have just been resting today in our tent. Harry did a little washing this morning & a few odds & ends, but he was taking it easy too most of the morning & all the afternoon. Mr. Tuckfield the Station Master is a nice fellow, & so delighted to have us here. We shall start for the Katherine tomorrow morning as soon as possible after breakfast.

Sunday 10th

We left the "Elsie" at 10, & arrived in camp on "The Duck Pond" at about 3, having done 20 miles. We passed close by a bitter spring, the water of which is quite bitter, it was off the road, so we did not go to it. This has seemed as unlike a Sunday as it is possible to be. I don't believe any of the party have remembered once what day it was except Harry & me, & then it's _we_ have only recalled it to one another in astonishment.

Monday 11th

We left camp at 8 & arrived without any stoppages at camp on a nice waterhole at 1/4 to 2. We passed a hill called Providence, a little hill about 30 ft high and not more than 2 or 300 yds round, where a party of men were camped during the wet season some years ago. All round the hill was water, & for 3 weeks or more they were detained there. Three of the men died & nearly all the horses. We did about 23 miles today.

Tuesday 12th

Left camp at 1/4 to 8 and arrived in camp at Bacon's Swamp at about 1/4 to 1, having come 20 miles. Riding along today we saw an ant bed fully 18 ft high, but not more than 20 ft round, in the shape of a sugar loaf. Lately we have seen some very prettily shaped beds, more like a castle with numerous towers than anything else. We shall get to the "Katherine" tomorrow afternoon I am thankful to say. I am feeling so very unwell, that I am afraid I should be knocked up if there were many more days of this. We have made a few Johnnie cakes of the last of our flour for breakfast tomorrow & we ate the last of our beef & sugar this evening, so it is time we got to our journey's end. The poor horses too are almost done.

Thursday 14th

We arrived safely at the Katherine yesterday at about 1/2 past 2 having come 25 miles. It was very hot riding in the sun so we were delighted to get in. Mr. & Mrs. Murray welcomed us most warmly & are doing everything to make us comfortable. Last night (there being no spare room) I slept with Mrs. M. & Harry & Mr. M. slept on the floor in the office, but today we have come into a little verandah room on the side of the house, the assistant's room really, but Mr. Johns & Mr. Kemp will make the store their quarters while we are here. Mrs. Murray has 3 children here, & the eldest a girl is in Adelaide. The house is nice & comfortable inside, but the building itself is a very poor affair. They are bringing in timber to build a new house, & then this will be turned into stores etc. This afternoon when it got a little cooler at about 4 the gentlemen took us out for a row on the river, which is close to the station.[68] We could only go a little distance owing to shallow water. Yesterday afternoon Mr. Giles[69] (the manager of a Station "Springvale"[70] about 7 miles from here) came over on business. He has his wife at the Station, but she did not come with him.[71] He asked Harry if we would go & stay with him before we leave for Port Darwin.

---

68 The Katherine River.
69 Alfred Giles was born in England in 1846. He gathered vast experience of the Northern Territory by participating in the exploratory expedition which prepared the way for the Overland Telegraph Line construction party. His experience of that expedition is recorded in his account *Exploring in the 'Seventies and the Construction of the Overland Telegraph Line*, originally published in Adelaide in 1926. Thereafter he spend many years establishing and managing cattle stations in the Northern Territory on behalf of Dr. W. B. Browne. Among them were three which play a role in Creaghe's diary, namely Springvale, Delamere Downs and Newcastle Waters. Giles died in Adelaide in 1931.
70 Springvale, the second station in the Territory, was one of several owned by Dr W. B. Browne and managed by Alfred Giles, was located on the Katherine River, some 13 kilometres west of Katherine
71 Mary Sprigg, the daughter of Henry Lorenzo Sprigg, had married Alfred Giles in February 1880.

Friday 15th

Oh! dear I wish we were down in Sydney or anywhere out of this place. I am perfectly wretched, being unwell & out of sorts altogether. Everything goes wrong somehow.

Saturday 16th

This afternoon we drove in the buggy (Mr. & Mrs. Murray, the 2 children, Mr. Kemp, Harry & I) to what they call "The big reach" a deep stretch of water about 14 miles long, where they keep one of their 2 boats, & had a very pleasant row, & returned just in time for tea.

Sunday 17th

Harry went & brought the horses in this morning to attend to some of their backs. This afternoon I made some tea cakes & Harry & I went for 2 short strolls in the afternoon & evening. The first stroll took us upon a camp of blacks mostly lubras. They are never allowed into the station for various reasons. We did not go across to them, they were on an opposite bank, but as long as they are so close to the station, there is no fear of their touching anyone, though they are not to be trusted any distance away.

Monday 18th

All day we did nothing particular, lying down & reading mostly. This evening after tea, Harry, Mr. Kemp & I went for a row on the river for an hour or so. Mr. Murray & Mr. Johns were afraid of catching fever on the river in the night air. We enjoyed the pull immensely, it was such a lovely moonlight night. Mrs. Murray had the baby to put to sleep so she couldn't come. Mr. Kemp goes back to the Daly tomorrow & Mr. Johns is going out on the line for a few days also.

Tuesday 19th

After a good deal of delay Mr. Johns & Mr. Kemp made a start at about 1/2 past 11. This afternoon I went into the kitchen for a while to do a little cooking, there being fresh meat for the first time since we came. Harry & Mr. Murray went for a ride the latter part of the afternoon. This evening we sat & talked out in the verandah.

Wednesday 20th

It being the Queen's anniversary to the Throne,[72] Mr. Murray was off duty all day, so we went over to the Giles' cattle Station 7 miles distant in the afternoon. Mr. & Mrs. Giles are nice kind hospitable people, no children.[73] They have a nice vegetable garden & any amount of banana trees, cotton, chili, paupau apple, etc. We stayed there till sundown when we had a very pleasant drive home in the moonlight. Mrs. Giles begged us to go & stay with them for a few days, so we are going back with Mr. Giles tomorrow, when he comes with the buggy. Mr. Giles asked Harry to take the management of his station for a few months while he is away on business, we have not decided yet whether we shall or not. We met a fellow named Hughes[74] there, he is helping Mr. Giles on the station.

Friday 22nd

One letter from Katie & a paper from Home. Yesterday Mr. Giles came over in the afternoon & took us back after the mail came in. Mr. Johns returned just after luncheon. We did not get to Springvale until after 7, so by the time tea was over we had only time to skim over the southern papers which had come by the afternoon's mail when we retired for the night. This house is built of stone with 2 rooms. Outside there is the kitchen & another little room which Mr.

---

72 Queen Victoria had ascended the throne in 1837. In 1883 she was just four years short of her Golden Jubilee.

73 In an article published in the *North Queensland Register* of 9 January 1932, Alfred Giles wrote under the sub-heading "First Lady Explorer": "To-day, 20th June, 1883, Mr. and Mrs. Creaghe came to Springvale. They are members of Mr. Ernest Favenc's exploring expedition. They have come on ahead from Powell's Creek, where they left Messrs. Favenc and Lindsay Crawford to finish the exploration. Mrs. Creaghe has ridden the whole distance on horseback and is undoubtedly the first lady to tackle exploring in Australia."

74 In his 1932 article in the *North Queensland Register* Alfred Giles wrote of Hughes: "In May, 1883, I engaged Mr. C.W. Hughes to act for me during my frequent absences from the station. Mr. Hughes later married a daughter of the late Mr. Maurice Holtze who was for a number of years superindentent of the Darwin Botanical Gardens and, later on, Director of the Adelaide Botanic gardens. He imported, while in Darwin, many eastern plants and tropical fruits and so laid the foundation of the present flourishing gardens.. He was highly esteemed as a botanist and director of the Adelaide gardens. Mr. Hughes now lives, I believe, on Kangaroo Island [...]."

Giles & Harry occupy. Mrs. Giles & I sleep together. Mrs. Giles has only been married about 3 years, but is over 33 years of age. She is nice, but quiet.

This afternoon we went down to the boat to go out for a pull, but the boat had been out of the water for some days so it leaked too much for us to use it today. Mr. Giles & Harry filled it with water, so it will be ready tomorrow. Mrs.Giles & I went for a walk down the river, & returned just before teatime. The mail bag went today, but neither of us wrote, there is too much to tell them all in writing, so we will wait till we see them.

Saturday 23rd

Today has been very warm again, it seems as though we were not going to have any cool weather. In the cool of the afternoon we went out in the boat to a nice place for a bathe, & Mr. Giles & Harry left us there, & we had a delightful bathe, & returned walking just in time for tea. Harry has decided not to take the management of this Station, he is afraid of this climate for me. I am very glad, this bush life is not pleasant by any means.

Sunday 24th

Today we did nothing but read & lie down until the cool of the evening when we went & sat in the garden under the banana trees until tea time. This evening Harry read the Church Service, it was so nice, we 4 round the table. This has been more like a Sunday than any since we left Sydney. Mr. Giles is even more strict than Harry about doing nothing secular on this day. He is a very good man; it is quite a treat to be in a house with religious people once more.

Monday 25th

The blacks were washing all the morning & Mrs. Giles was occupied superintending it. In the cool of the afternoon we all went for a nice row about 2 miles up the river, & returned home just in time for tea. Mr. Giles is going away at the end of the week for a fortnight or so, & Mrs. Giles wants us to remain with her while he is away as there is a Mr. Hughes lives here, who is away for a few days at present, but

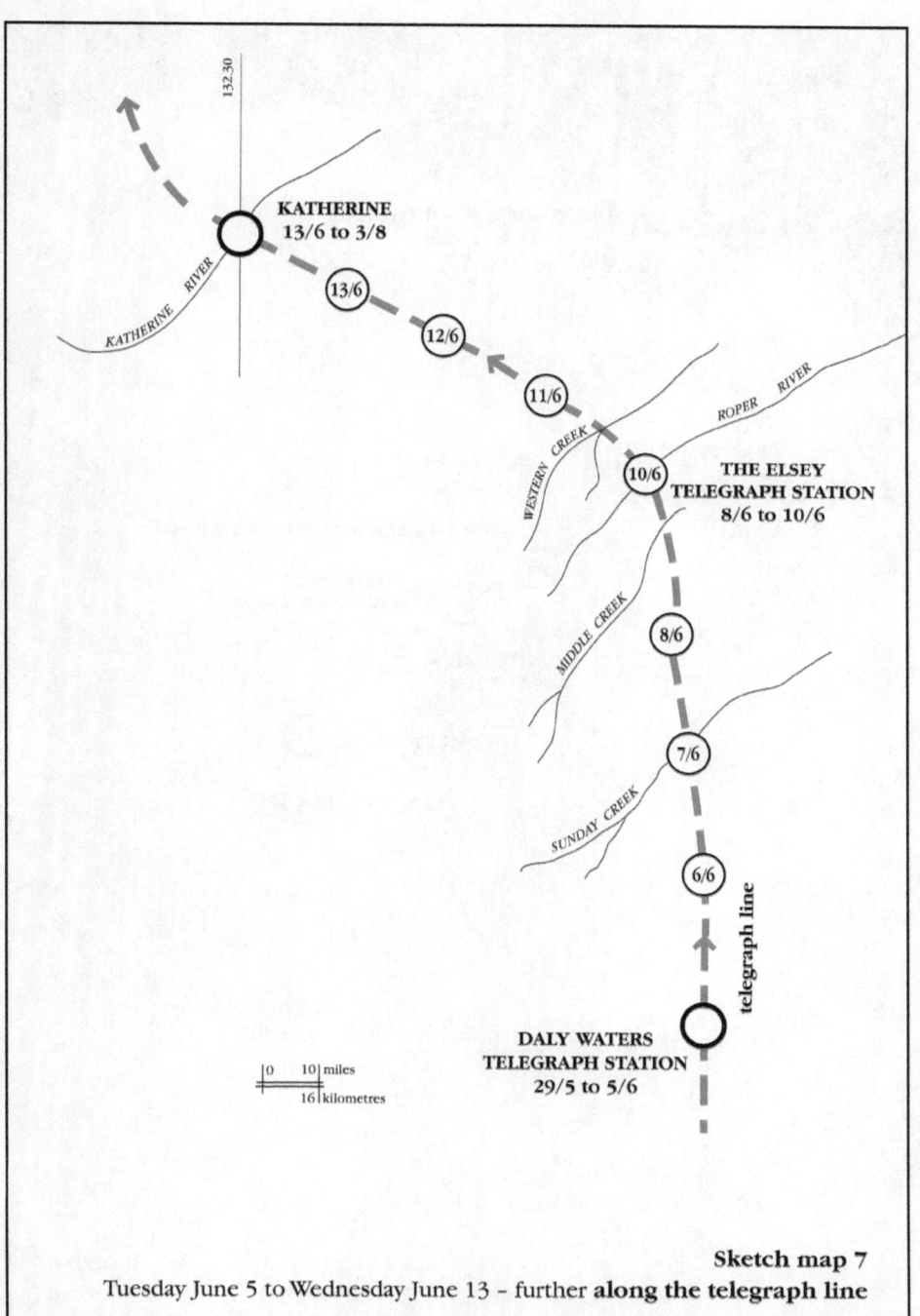

Sketch map 7
Tuesday June 5 to Wednesday June 13 – further **along the telegraph line**

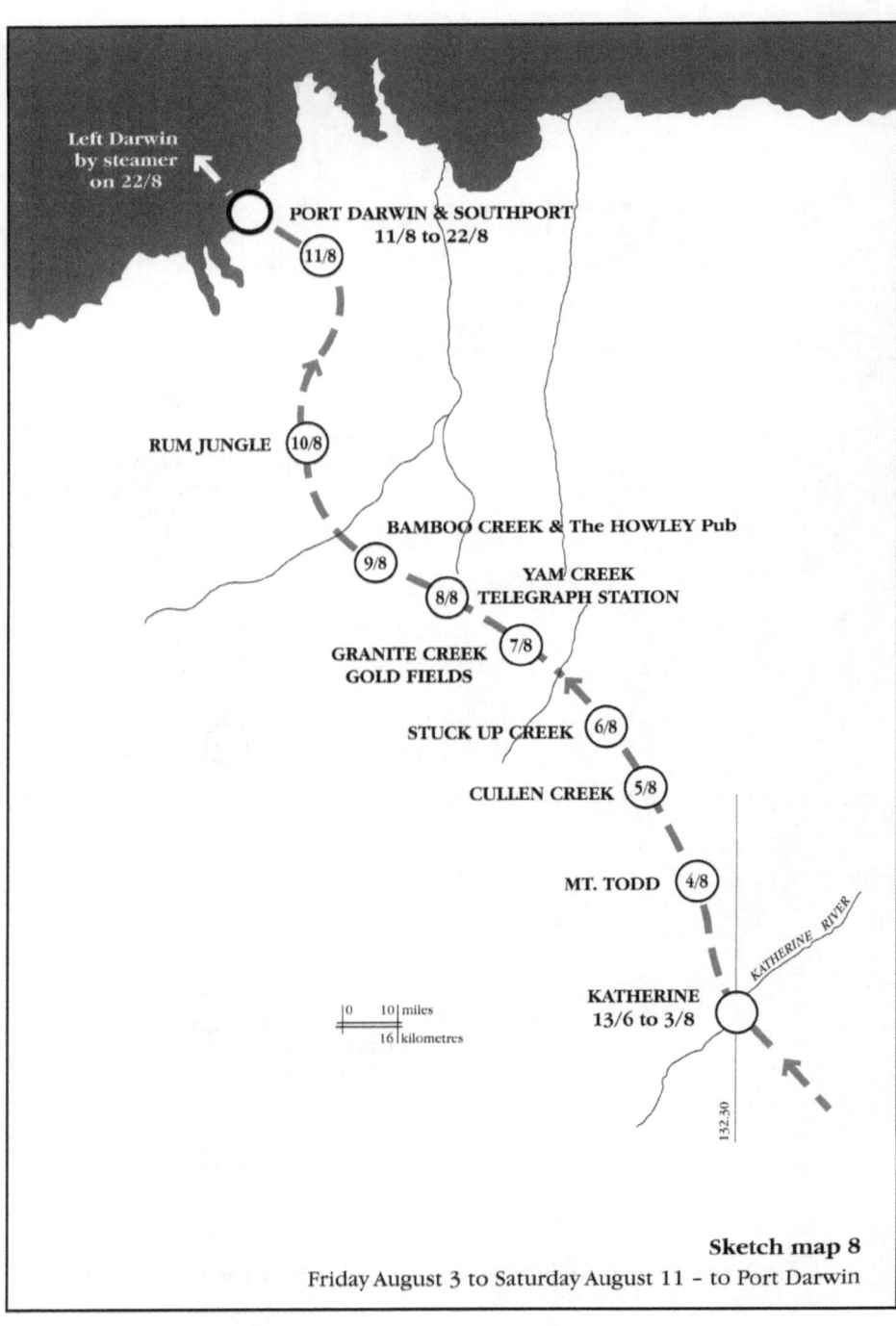

will be back before he goes & she cannot stay alone in the house with him, he being a young bachelor.

Tuesday 26th

Did nothing particular except iron in the morning. Slept after dinner until late in the afternoon, then went for a stroll through the garden with Harry. He & Mr. Giles rode out this morning to look for the buggy horses to go for a drive this afternoon, but did not find them after being out till 1/2 past 2. We had dinner alone, Mrs. G. & I.

Wednesday 27th

This morning we did nothing particular, I was lying down nearly all the time not being well. This afternoon Harry drove me to the Murrays' to tell them we would not be back till the end of next week. We returned about 1/2 past 6. just in time to get ready for tea. It was very hot & dusty going to the Station, but coming back it was nice & cool. We passed a mob of 1800 cattle on their way to "Glencoe" a Station about 100 miles from here. They have come from N.S.W. & have been 17 months on the road.

Thursday 28th

Mr. Hughes came back today after dinner. We went for a drive this afternoon, first to see a spring, which is most peculiar. Where the spring is, is a large mound covered all over with pandanus or corkscrew palms, & in the centre of this mound is a spout of water always running, just below the spout is a little pond, then the water runs away in little streams down the mound & along the flat a little way. We then went round a large "billibung" (a pond) covered with immense waterlily leaves & a few pink lilies. The leaves are immense round things, larger than the largest wash hand basin & the flowers are large dark pink, they look lovely all over the water. The Port Darwin mail arrived this afternoon, no steamer from the South being in, we got no news of any consequence. A very high wind has been blowing all day, but went down before dark. The wind was not pleasant as the air was no cooler.

Friday 29th

Did nothing particular all day. Had music all the evening. Harry & I went for a short stroll along the river bank in the afternoon.

Saturday 30th

This afternoon Harry rode over to the Murrays' & brought back the only 2 of our horses that have not been sold. Mrs. Giles & I went for a bathe in the river when it got a little cool. A high wind blowing all day, warm. No news of Favenc yet.

Sunday 1st

We spent a quiet pleasant day reading until late in the afternoon, when Harry & I went & sat under the banana trees, & the other 3 went for a walk. I didn't feel well enough to go further than the garden. We had service again this evening, Harry reading it. We finished up with Sankey's hymns. Mr. Hughes also appreciates service on Sundays so we are a united party at Springvale. High wind as usual, coming up at 10 & going down about 5.

Monday 2nd

Mr. Giles intended to have started to another Station of his, 80 miles from here, & was busy all the morning, but owing to a mob of 180 horses just having arrived at the Katherine & he wanting to buy some, he got Harry to go & purchase for him, which he did. He came back soon after we had had dinner, to get some help in bringing them back, & he persuaded Mr. Giles to wait & see them, so he will go tomorrow instead. I did nothing all day, but lie down & read, too seedy for anything else. Windy & warm.

Tuesday 3rd

The horses came at about 9, & Mr. Giles went off to "Delemere" soon after. Harry had neuralgia[75] all day very badly, he is slightly better this evening. This climate is knocking him up completely. Windy & warm.

Wednesday 4th

Harry's neuralgia has been better today. We intended going for a row, & to shoot some wild ducks, but when we got into the boat, we found it leaking so much, owing to its having been out of the water for some days that we had to put it off. Windy & warm as usual.

Thursday 5th

This morning we did nothing particular, we had dinner at 12 an hour earlier than usual, & went over to the Murrays' in the buggy, all 4 of us, Harry driving. The road was too rough for enjoyment of the drive. We got home just before tea time. No news of Favenc yet. The mail came in today, but there was no southern mail.

---

75 Pain stemming from the nerves.

Friday 6th

Mr. Murray had some races up at the Station this morning, to which Harry went directly after breakfast, & returned at 1/2 past 4, after which we all went for a row for an hour or so. Mr. Hughes could not leave here, as 2 of the men wanted to go to see the races; I could have ridden with Harry if I had liked, but I didn't feel inclined for a 20 miles ride. The race course is 3 1/2 miles from the "Katherine". Windy as usual. Harry has just received a memo from the Telegraph Station from Daly Waters to the following effect. A black fellow brought in there in a very dilapidated condition, a note from Favenc 100 miles or so from the Daly to say they had suffered for want of water, having been 3 nights without it, & had to leave their packs behind. Owing to the letter's being so much destroyed, nothing more is known. McFee, who went out from the Daly when we were there has had to turn back for want of water; he went out to bring a mob of cattle over from the McArthur; they will have to stay on that river till rain comes.

Saturday 7th

Did nothing particular (our usual occupation). "A paper yabber" came over from the "Katherine" to tell us the Murrays would be here for dinner tomorrow. A "paper yabber" is what the niggers call a letter. White people employ them as messengers, & very faithful ones they are. The niggers have a stick, which they make a slit in, in which the letter is placed, & in wet or fine weather this letter is taken every care of, in wet weather, if it is going a long distance, the nigger sleeps over it to keep it dry, & when journeying wraps it in leaves (tea-tree or paper bark). They are repaid for bringing it by a fig of tobacco, which completely satisfies them. Windy, but much cooler than usual.

Sunday 8th

The Murrays & Mr. Johns came to dinner & stayed till 5. this afternoon. Mr. Murray heard from the P&T Office[76] in Pt. Darwin that a number of our letters had just arrived from Hong Kong, having been mis-carried, so that accounts for our getting no letters. How Katie's escaped I don't know.

---

76 Post and Telegraph Office.

Monday 9th

Have done nothing all day but read. I shall be delighted when this aimless idle life is over, & we are once more on our journey. Cool & windy.

Tuesday 10th

Mr. Giles returned early this afternoon from "Delemere", so we shall go back to the "Katherine" tomorrow. Cool & windy all day.

Wednesday 11th

Mr. Giles drove us up to the "Katherine" this afternoon after an early dinner. We all came in the buck-board.[77] It only has a seat for 2, but Harry sat on the board behind, & got a delightful jolting. Mr. Murray went to meet a Mr. McMinn,[78] the Resident of Port Darwin, who is coming here for a few days, they will arrive tomorrow evening most likely. The new station is being put up by chinamen, one of them having the contract. It is only just begun since Monday.

Thursday 12th

The mailman arrived with heaps of letters, but the latest is dated the end of April, so the news is very old.[79] Mr. Murray sent word along the line that he won't be in till tomorrow. No wind today, very warm.

---

77 A basic carriage consisting of a large plank on wheels.
78 Gilbert Rotherdale McMinn (1841–1924), an Irishman, was for some fourteen months in 1883–1884 Acting Government Resident in the Northern Territory, and as such the South Australian government's leading administrator in the north. He knew the territory well from earlier work there as a surveyor; he had also supervised the construction of part of the Overland Telegraph Line. His brother, William McMinn, also spent time in the Northern Territory, but his main legacy is in Adelaide, where as an architect he designed a number of prominent buildings, including the University of Adelaide. See V.T. O'Brien, "Gilbert Rotherdale McMinn", in *Northern Territory Dictionary of Biography*, Vol. One: To 1945. Edited by David Carment, Robyn Maynard and Alan Powell, Darwin: NTU Press, 1990, pp. 202–203, and Goerge E. Loyau, *Notable South Australians*, Adelaide: n.p., 1885.
79 It was on this day that Creaghe wrote to her father. The text of what remains of that letter is reproduced here after the diary.

Friday 13th

Mr. McMinn & Mr. Murray arrived at 2 o'clock, with Harry & Mr. Johns who went to meet them. Mr. McMinn is a surveyor, but is acting Resident in Mr. Price's absence.[80] The mailman stays here till tomorrow morning, when he goes back again. Very warm. Wrote this evening to Papa, & Home (Laura).[81]

Saturday 14th

We all went out for a row when it got a little cool, did nothing else all day. Very warm.

Sunday 15th

Mr. Murray & Mr. McMinn drove down to Spring Vale in the morning, & returned at tea time. Mrs. Murray, Mr. Johns, Harry & I went to the mouth of an immense cave a short distance from here, we did not go down to explore it as it was very dirty & pitch dark. It has not seemed much like Sunday. We were overjoyed to get a wire from the Daly in the afternoon to say Favenc had arrived at dinner time, so we shall soon be on our way down. They lost 2 horses, & have been living on a handful of flour a day for the last 10 days.

Monday 16th

I was very poorly all day & was lying down from breakfast till tea time. Harry rode to Spring Vale this morning & returned for dinner, to go to the "big reach", I being unwell Mrs. Murray stayed at home, but the others went & the 2 girls. Mr. Hughes came up with the buck board to take Mr. McMinn to Pine Creek tomorrow.

Tuesday 17th

Mr. Murray & Harry went out to look for horses all the morning & returned at 3, without having found any. Mr. McMinn & Mr. Hughes went at about 1/2 past 9 this morning. Sent a telegram to Papa as Mr. Murray offered to send for 3 instead of 5/-.

---

80 Edward W. Price had departed the position of Government Resident earlier in 1883. He was eventually replaced by J. Langdon Parsons in May 1884.
81 Matilda Lauretta Creaghe, Harry's younger sister by 10 years. "Home" here means Ireland.

Spring Vale Station 1883
State Library of South Australia

David Lindsay ca. 1880
State Library of South Australia

Wednesday 18th

This afternoon we went for a delightful drive & scramble over some high rocks about 2 miles from here. We got a number of pretty red seeds about the rocks. We all went. The rocks in some parts are most peculiar. They look as though they had been placed by human hands. Some are about 8 ft high, 5 or 6 yards apart, & in shape of a cone, consisting of small rocks placed one on top of the other, all separate. In appearance the whole looks like a ruin of an old Roman City.

Thursday 19th

We walked to the cave we went to the mouth of on Sunday this afternoon, & explored it. We went into 3 chambers which were pitch dark, we took a lighted candle & the inside was very fine. There were lovely pieces of petrified water hanging down in all directions. When we got home the mail had arrived & I got letters from Louie & Minnie. It is very warm all day.

Friday 20th

Mr. Lindsay[82] & Cuthbertson arrived this morning on their way out on an exploring trip. They are very nice, & gentlemen. The latter has been 7 times round the world. The summer seems to have commenced & I feel the want of cool clothing very much.

---

82 David Lindsay, born in Goolwa in South Australia in 1856, was a surveyor by training and had worked in the Northern Territory since 1878. By the time of his meeting with Creaghe he had resigned his government post to go into private practice, possibly in the hope of making the most of the growth at that time in the pastoral industry. However, it was in the service of the South Australian government that he explored Arnhem Land in 1883, and he may well have been on his way there when he came across Creaghe. That expedition triggered a passion for exploration which he pursued later in the decade. His greatest success should have been as the leader of a major expedition financed by Sir Thomas Elder. The expedition would have complemented Favenc's work east of the Telegraph Line by exploring territory to its west. Alas, after leaving Adelaide in 1891 the party encountered drought conditions; acrimony broke out in the group, so that only a remnant finally made it to Geraldton in early 1892, where Elder abandoned the expedition. Nonetheless Lindsay remained a vigorous champion of the development of the Northern Territory. See P.F. Donovan, "David Lindsay (1856–1922) Explorer, Surveyor and Northern Territory Apologist", *South Australiana* 18, 2 (Sept. 1979). and "David Lindsay", in *Northern Territory Dictionary of Biography*, Vol. One: To 1945. Edited by David Carment, Robyn Maynard and Alan Powell, Darwin: NTU Press, 1990, pp, 182–84.

Saturday 21st

This afternoon Mr. Murray had a sale of a man's horses who died here a few weeks ago, to which Mr. & Mrs. Giles & some of their men came. Mr. Lindsay & Cuthbertson went to their camp (4 miles from here) tonight as they wanted to get clean clothes, etc. They will return tomorrow & make a start on their trip on Monday. Just before bedtime Mr. Murray, Harry & I went about a 1/4 mile from the Station to see the niggers corroboring.[83] We heard their noise while outside, so went to see the fun. There were about 10 there, 3 of them being station boys. When they are here they have shirt & trousers given them, but there they were as the wild ones, naked. We heard from the "Elsie"[84] of Favenc's arrival there this afternoon, so he will probably be here on Tuesday.

Sunday 22nd

Mr. Lindsay & Cuthbertson went to Springvale before evening here today, & didn't get here till after 2. We had a little excitement during the afternoon over the capture of an emu by one of the dogs. It was killed before I got to the scene of action. The "death" was only a 100 yds or so from the house. This evening when it was dark we all went up to the niggers camp & saw a bigger corrobory than last night. Mr. Murray told them yesterday to have a "big fellow corrobory" tonight, so there were 16 or 17 niggers tonight. There were a number not there & no gins. In this part the gins never show themselves unless they are taken by surprise. Mr. Lindsay & Cuthbertson went to their camp at 10, to get ready to make an early start tomorrow.

---

83 That is, staging a corroboree.
84 That is, the Elsey Telegraph Station.

Monday 23rd

Mr. Foulchie[85] arrived from Port Darwin shortly after dinner. He is the Inspector of Police (white) there & is on his way to form a new police barracks at the "Elsie". At tea time there was another arrival a Mr. Gordon, who has come over from Queensland with cattle for some station near here.[86] There are 3000 in all, & they are in 3 mobs, one mob 4 days behind the first & the 3rd 6 days behind the 2nd. Lindsay & Cuthbertson called here on their way out this morning. They have 32 horses in all. Two white & 2 black fellows. The 2 gentlemen stayed to lunch, & left directly after. The pack horses went on some time before luncheon.

Tuesday 24th

This morning three of the gentlemen went out in the boat for Mr. Foulchie to take a photo of the station, he is an amateur photographer. Harry stayed at home. In the afternoon they all except Mrs. Murray & me, went to the "Big reach" also to photograph. They came home just in time for tea.

Wednesday 25th

Mr. Foulchie went to Springvale this morning to take a photo of the place, & will be back tomorrow. Harry went there this afternoon to

---

85 Paul Heinrich Matthias Foelsche (Creaghe later spells his name correctly) was born in Hamburg in 1831 and migrated to South Australia in 1854. He joined the South Australian Police Force in 1856 and served for some time in Strathalbyn. He arrived in Port Darwin in 1870 as officer-in-charge of the first police detachment in the Northern Territory. He was also something of an amateur photographer and anthropologist of note. After retirement in 1904 he remained in the Northern Territory, where he died in 1914, just a few months before the outbreak of the Great War. His name is perpetuated in Mount Foelsche, Foelsche River, Foelsche Headland, Eucalyptus Foelscheana and Darwin's Foelsche Street. See Gordon Reid, "Paul Heinrich Matthias Foelsche", in *Northern Territory Dictionary of Biography*, Vol. One: To 1945. Edited by David Carment, Robyn Maynard and Alan Powell, Darwin: NTU Press, 1990, 107–108.

86 The transcription of the diary adds here the clarification "for Fisher and Lyons at Victoria Downs". Victoria River Downs was owned by Fisher and Lyons.

make final arrangements about going to Palmerston (Pt. Darwin).[87] We go with the Giles's on Thursday. Favenc & Crawford will be here tomorrow we expect.

Thursday 26th

Favenc & Crawford arrived at 4 P.M. looking very thin & black. They saw no niggers all the time they were out strange to say. Mr. Foelsche (Mr. Foulchie) came during the afternoon, & the mailman also. No Southern mail.

Friday 27th

Mr. Foelsche went away directly after breakfast to take some photos on the Edith[88] on his way back to Palmerston, Mr. Murray & Crawford went after him later, to camp tonight with him. We were all going, only Favenc & Harry had to settle some business, & couldn't go. It was cooler today.

Saturday 28th

Favenc went away with the mailman this morning, we start on Thursday with the Giles's. It has been a little cooler today, but a disagreeable wind blowing. Harry went with Favenc to the Giles, & brought Mr. G. back.

Sunday 29th

Very windy all day, so nice & cool. Mr. Murray & Crawford came back this evening. Maudie & Mr. Johns went to meet them, & they all returned for tea. Mr. Murray has just been playing some waltz's, while I am on my own. It is the first time I have ever been in a house where secular music is played on Sunday. We shall both be thoroughly delighted to get amongst our own set again.

---

87 There had been a number of unsuccessful attempts to establish a European settlement on the coast of the Northern Territory. After the 1867 failure of Escape Cliffs in Adams Bay, Port Darwin was chosen as the most appropriate site. The settlement there was named Palmerston but was often referred to by the name of its harbour, Port Darwin.

88 The Edith River, which crosses the Telegraph Line north of Katherine.

Monday 30th

Harry took the horses Mr. Giles bought from us on Saturday to "Springvale" this afternoon. Mr. Johns & Crawford leave tomorrow for Palmerston. We shall all go south by the same boat I expect.

Tuesday 31st

Crawford & Mr. Johns started late this morning. We have been busy packing, & getting everything washed & ironed, to start tomorrow morning.

Southport Police Station 1879
Photograph by Paul Foelsche
State Library of South Australia

Wednesday 1st

The Murrays & we came down to luncheon, they went back at 4. Mr. Giles cannot manage to get away till Friday, but it doesn't matter as the steamer does not leave Palmerston for a fortnight.

Thursday 2nd

Have done nothing all day. Mr. & Mrs. Giles busy packing. Mr. Hughes got fever this morning after breakfast, & has not been out of his room since.

Friday 3rd

The horses were not brought in till 1 o'clock, so we have only come to the "10 Mile" (10 miles from "Spring Vale"). Our party consists of the Giles's, ourselves, & Ah Gow a chinaman,[89] & Bonda a black boy. Mr. & Mrs. Giles are driving in their big wagon & we are in the little buck-board. Ah Gow is in the wagon & Bonda is riding. We got into camp at 1/2 past 4. It has been very warm all day, & is still. Had a nice bathe.

Saturday 4th

We left the Ten Mile at 1/4 past 9, & went over a most frightfully stony road for 14 miles when we camped at an almost dry creek for lunch. It was very hot. We are glad to get out of the buggies & sit under the shade of a tree. We left again at 4 & got into camp at Mt. Tod[90] at about 1/2 past 5 having come about 20 miles in all. Last night we had a slight shower during the night but hardly enough to lay the dust.

Sunday 5th

We had a severe storm of rain in the night & every thing was soaking this morning. Fortunately Harry's trousers & my dress we had under our heads for pillows, so they were dry but everything else

---

89 The transcription of the diary adds here the clarification "cook".
90 Mt Todd, located just east of the Telegraph Line, and named after Charles Todd who, as South Australia's postmaster-general and superintendent of telegraphs, played a leading role in the construction of the line.

was wringing. We couldn't start until they were dry, so we hung them all up the Giles's clothes & all, the first thing when we got up. The sun came out at 9, so everything was dry by 11 o'clock so we had a little lunch & started at 12, getting into camp on the "Cullen" (creek) at 1/2 past 5. having come 19 miles. There is a camp of niggers camped close here, we can hear them corroboring, from the noise they must be a large mob. It is the same tribe Bonda comes from & he went over to them after tea, but had to come to the camp to sleep. It has been hotter than ever today, a steamy heat after the rain. Mrs. G. & I had a bathe in a horrid hole.

Monday 6th
We had a cooler night – but today it is very hot. At about 1 we passed a broken down dray of Mr. Giles, so we went on a mile to water & camped while Mr. G. went to Pine Creek to see about new wheels. We came 11 miles instead of 24 as we had intended. We are only 4 miles from Pine Creek. In the Creek we are on, there are 4 chinamen digging for gold. We are now in Gold country. They tell us they get from 8 to 15/- per week but Mr. Giles thinks they get more only they are afraid we will interfere with their monopoly of the place so won't tell us the real quantity. This camp is called "Stuck Up" camp. Mr. G. brought back some English potatoes, the first I have had for 8 months.

Tuesday 7th
We packed up this morning while Harry went in the buck-board to where the dray is broken down. to get some feed for the horses. We all made a start at about 1/2 past 9. We stopped a mile the other side of Pine Crk at Janson's, the owner of a fine gold mine. He shewed us over the works but for want of water they are not crushing just now. Janson is a nice kind German. He pressed us to take some quartz out of a dish of specimens he had. He has a nice little log cottage of 2 or 3 rooms & has a chinaman to cook. We came on at 1/2 past 11 & camped at a waterhole for lunch at 2 we left again at 4, & arrived in camp about 1/2 past 5. having come 21 miles in all. It has been very hot again all day. Had a delightful bathe in a lovely rocky hole this

evening & did some washing. This camp is "Granite Creek" from the numerous rocks of that stone all round.

Wednesday 8th

Left camp at 1/2 past 9 & stopped for lunch at a number of small waterholes about 11 miles on. The road was very heavy so we had to come slowly. Arrived at Yam Crk at 4, 6 miles from the lunch camp. This is a nice cool looking house (the telegraph Station kept by Mr. Kelsey & a young brother). They pressed us to stay all night so we are doing so. Our steamer leaves a day earlier than we expected & we have 90 miles still to go so we must make great haste. Very hot all day. Yam Crk or The Shackle as it is properly called, has only the narrow track through it & has 4 houses. As far as we could see; Public house, Police Station, Gold Warden's & telegraph Station. The road was pretty good today, but heavy & very dusty.

Thursday 9th

We left at 11 from the "Shackle", came as far as the Howley (a Public house) & camped about a mile from it. When we came out of Yam Crk we passed a large gold field with 50 to 100 chinese working in small claims. We passed during the day numerous chinamen on foot evidently going to the gold field. The heat was intense & the dust something frightful. We could not see a yard in front of us for miles the dust was so thick. We left the Howley at about 4 & came through Bridge Crk, a public house & store comprising the village. The woman in charge died there this morning, there were several people there, some making the coffin. The mornings stage was 21 miles, the afternoons 7. It was a good road so we came very quickly, getting into camp on Bamboo Crk just before dark. We left Ah Gow at The Shackle, we being in a hurry, so wanting as light a load as possible. We also left the Giles' tent, it was such a heavy one, so Mrs. G. & I are going to camp together & the 2 gentlemen outside. We passed a regular forest of bamboos this afternoon.

Friday 10th

Left camp at 9 & travelled 18 miles along a good but very dusty road.

Had lunch 1/4 of a mile from the Adelaide River Pub., there is only one other building viz. police station. Mr. Foelsche who has been taking views all the way down since he left the Katherine caught us up there, & we chatted with him for an hour or so & left the Adelaide at 3. We hurried as fast as we could & over a very heavy road & got to Rum Jungle just at dark. There is a Public House & one settler in this place. We had tea at the hotel & will have breakfast. Mr. & Mrs. Giles are going to sleep inside, but we have pitched our tent, the rooms in the house are so close. Yesterday we passed the place where the Blacks had murdered 4 chinamen a year ago, and today we passed the spot where they killed a white man some short time ago. We have been passing such enormous ant beds, ranging from 15 to 20 ft high.

Saturday 11th

We left camp at 10, & travelled 14 miles & camped for lunch at a lovely place, a river with lovely thick tropical foliage in abundance. It was very hot & we did not start on till 1/2 past 4, we came the remaining 14 miles pretty quickly considering the heavy road & got to Southport[91] at a little before dark. We are staying at the Telegraph Station. Mr. & Mrs. Johnson have a nice large house & nicely furnished and a number of chinese servants. We have come to the end of our journey (overland). After dinner which we had at 8, served in good style, Mr. Gray & Mr. Blightson, or some such name, came in & stayed all night. The time passed so quickly that when we thought of going to bed we found it was nearly 1 o'clock. We have been passing several drays for the last 2 days, & also chinese on foot. We find the steamer is not expected till Friday, so we are going to stay here till Tuesday.

Sunday 12th

Very hot all day. This morning the gentlemen read the Southern papers that came by yesterday's mail from Pt. Darwin. In the cool of the afternoon, we all took a walk through the city (!) of Southport. It consists of 6 or 8 chinese stores & one English, at which one can

---

91 A settlement south of Palmerston on the southern arm of Port Darwin.

get nothing one wants. The houses are all built of corrugated iron, which the inhabitants prefer to any other material, as it soon gets cool after the heat of the day is over.

Monday 13th

Mr. Foelsche arrived this afternoon & is staying all night. It was slightly cooler today. We did some of our packing & sent it down to the steam launch which is only 5 minutes walk from here.

Tuesday 14th

We left the Johnsons' at 8 o'clock after an earlier breakfast than usual. The little steam-launch was waiting for us, so we left immediately, & arrived at Port Darwin at 11. after a rather monotonous trip. The river on either side is one mass of mangroves. There are plenty of aligators, but we didn't see any. Palmerston is a nice looking little place, & the residence can be seen on the point at a good distance from shore. Mr. McMinn sent a boat off for us, & had the phaeton at the landing (no wharf) to take us up to the Residence. This is a splendid bungalow house, with 8 or 9 large & lofty rooms, the floor of cement without carpets. The verandah is a very pretty one very wide & all round the house, with also a cement floor. After lunch the Giles's & we went into the town to do some shopping. We first went round the chinese quarters. Nearly all the shops are chinese, but there were not many curios to be seen. We got back at 4, & then Mr. McMinn took us for a nice drive. We went to the Government gardens (mostly fruit & vegetables, kept by chinese) & also to look over the new gaol about 2 miles from here. We got home just in time to dress for dinner, which is at 1/2 past 7. Harry & Mr. Giles were over at the Cable telegraph department. Harry was playing tennis with them when we returned. They have a nice lawn there for it, & the gentlemen seem very happy & comfortable. I haven't seen any of them yet. Mr. Knight the P.M. came in this morning for a short time. After dinner Mr. McMinn & I had some music, he playing the violin & I the American organ, there is no piano here at present.

Portrait of Paul Foelsche, Inspector, ca. 1880
State Library of South Australia

Cherry St. Southport ca. 1878
State Library of South Australia

Wednesday 15th

This morning we did nothing particular, this afternoon Harry & Mr. G. went over to the Cable office & played tennis, & I with Mr. McMinn went out in the Government yacht, besides us there were the two Miss Foelsches, Mr. Brydent, a Mr. Whitelaw, Mr. Little, Mr. Buckland. We returned in time to dress for dinner. After dinner we all went to see the Townhall (a building lately put up) & to get books from the library there. Mr. Baines the teller of the E&A Bank is the librarian, & we had a nice chat about music, he is passionately fond of it & sings well I believe. Mr. & Mrs. Favenc with Mr. Little came in while we were there. They are staying with the latter. We went to see the B.A.T.[92] also this evening.

Thursday 16th

No signs of the steamer this morning. We had invitations to a dance at Mr. Little's this evening, both Mrs. Giles & I refused, on the score of having no dresses. This afternoon Mr. Little wrote over again to say never mind dress, but come, so Mrs. G. went, but Harry & I stayed at home. Mr. McMinn lent me his phaeton, so Mrs. G. & I went for a nice drive to the gardens when it got cool in the afternoon. Mr. Baines came over for an hour or so during the evening, when the dance was going on. He said it was too hot for dancing, so he came to chat with us. Mr. Little's house is quite close, so we heard the music quite distinctly. Mr. & Mrs. G. came home early at a little after 10. Mr. McMinn did not come until much later. We did not wait up for him.

Friday 17th

The "Venice" won't be here for another 10 days. Mrs. Solomon[93] &

---

92 The building housing the British Australian Telegraph Company.
93 Alice Solomon was the wife of Vaiben Louis Solomon, an Adelaide-born Jew whose father had served as Mayor of Adelaide. The younger Solomon moved to the Northern Territory in 1873, where he was able to benefit from the gold-mining industry and establish wide-ranging business interests. In the year after Creaghe's visit the Solomons' house was described as "the most complete and substantial private residence Palmerston can boast of." See Suzanne Saunders, "Vaiben Louis Solomon", in *Northern Territory Dictionary of Biography, Vol. One: To 1945*. Edited by David Carment, Robyn Maynard and Alan Powell, Darwin: NTU Press, 1990, pp. 265–68.

Mrs. Hilson called on us this afternoon, & the latter has invited us all there tomorrow evening. We all went for a walk at 5 round the place & got back in time to dress for dinner. The 2 Miss Marches came in during the evening, Mr. McMinn had asked them last evening, as we are never at home in the afternoons. The "Feilung"[94] is expected in tomorrow.

Saturday 18th

This afternoon Mrs. Giles & I went to return Mrs. Favenc's & Mrs. Harvey's calls, but did not start till 5. as it was too hot. After dinner we went to Mrs. Hilson's & met there Mrs. Solomon, Mrs. Favenc, Miss Biddels, Messrs. Brightson, Craig, Baines, Ward, Solomon, Favenc & Mr. Hilson. We got home at 1/2 past 11. Everyone lives in the township, so we had no distance to walk. We slept from lunch time till 4. No "Feilung" yet.

Sunday 19th

Mr. Giles & I went to the only church in Palmerston, a Wesleyan Chapel, this morning. There were 9 persons in all present. Mr. Stuart is the minister, & such a poor preacher that it is no wonder people prefer staying at home in this hot climate. This evening Mrs. G. & Harry came too. The Church of E.[95] service in the evening & there were fully 3 dozen there. The building would hardly hold more than 50 comfortably, it is a little barn of a place. Mr. McMinn was not in when we returned but came soon after bringing Mr. Patti a B.A.T. man with him. B.A.T. stands for British & Australian Telegraph. We all slept all the afternoon. Everyone sleeps in the afternoons for 2 or 3 hrs every day in this place. Again no steamer.

Monday 20th

This morning Mrs. Giles & I went down to what is commonly called "The camp", the house where Mr. Ward & Baines & Whitelaw & one

---

94 According to Alfred Giles the vessel was the "Fee Sung", though Creaghe's recollection appears likely to be the more accurate, since "Feilung" means "flying dragon". As Creaghe reveals later, almost the entire crew was Chinese and might well have come from an Asian port before proceeding to the eastern coast of Australia.

95 Church of England, to which the Creaghes belonged.

other man live. They have the best piano in Palmerston (which is not saying much, for they are all wretched) & asked me to go & see it. They are out at work from 1/2 past 9 to 1/2 past 12, so we were undisturbed. After our usual siesta, Mr. McMinn took Mrs. G. & me for a drive round the race-course, the same drive we went the previous times, there is no other place to go, & coming home we returned the Marshs' call. We had a shower of rain this morning, just enough to make it hotter all day & not to lay the dust. No steamer come yet.

Tuesday 21st

The "Feilung" came in before breakfast this morning. Harry & I went on board to look at her, & found that she has only one cabin, but the Capt. offered us his, & the boat is remarkably clean, so we are going & Mrs. G. too. We leave here at 1/2 past 5 tomorrow morning. This afternoon, Mrs. G. & I returned Mrs. Solomon's & Foelsche's calls. It has been a little cooler all day. This evening we had quite a bevy of farewell visitors. Mr. Sierey, Mr. Whitelaw, Mr. Baines, Ward, Bernard, Stowe, & Buckland. I have forgotten to say that all the servants are chinese, there is not a woman in any house in Palmerston. The town is infested with niggers, having little or no clothing on. The men are employed at the stores for odd jobs.

Wednesday 22nd

We left the residence at 1/2 past 5, and came on board by the Custom's boat. We did not leave Port till after 7, so we need not have left our beds so early. We have been travelling very slowly owing to a strong head wind. The Pilot Mr. Marsh came about 60 miles with us.

Thursday 23rd

Still making very little progress. Mrs. G. is very ill & I am not very bright. This boat is almost entirely manned by chinese. Cook, stewards & all.

Friday 24th

Harry & I sleep on deck all night. The cabin is so close. Head wind still blowing.

Saturday 25th
Strong head wind blowing. We shall not get to Thursday Island till tomorrow night. The trip is generally done in 3 days.

Sunday 26th
Slept pretty well all day. Head wind blowing still.

Monday 27th
Arrived at Thursday Island this morning at about 10. Mr Chester & Jessie & Mr. Boor came on board, & we went back with the former & remained all night. Mrs. Chester is at home & is very pleasant. She is the daughter of an old Indian Officer named Lucas. Mrs. G. came with us.

Tuesday 28th
We left the Chesters' at 1/2 past 11. The steamer sailed at 1/2 past 12. We are getting along faster now, being in smooth water. We came through Albany Pass at about 4. We anchored at 9 for the night, not being able to procure a pilot, & the Capt. being new to this coast, he does not like to risk coming in the dark along the coast.

Wednesday 29th
We passed the "Hampshire" this afternoon, a British India boat, bound for Home, & also a light-ship. Anchored at 7 tonight.

Thursday 30th
Nice day, not much wind. Passed a light-ship this afternoon.

Friday 31st
We arrived in sight of Cooktown at dusk, but too late to go up to the wharf so we are anchored about a mile out. Mr. Milman the P.M.[96] an old friend of Harry's & 2 or 3 other gentlemen came on board.

---

96 Probably Post Master.

Chinese Market Gardeners NT ca. 1885
State Library of South Australia

Palmerston Telegraph Office and Residency ca. 1890
State Library of South Australia

Saturday 1st

The steamer came to the wharf at 11 or so, & we took Mrs. G. to see the town, & the chinese quarters. After tiffin[97] we went to see the Bauers' & found only Miss B. & the 3 little ones there. Mrs. B. & the others are at their plantation 30 miles away. We spent an hour with her then went on board the "Corea" which had just come in to see Capt. Lourie. After dinner Harry & I went again to spend the evening with the Bauers. Mr. Fritz Bauer the eldest son is there for a few days. We met also a Mr. Bostock & Mr. Warren. We got back to the ship at 11, after having spent a pleasant musical evening. We sent a telegram to Papa to say we were coming.

Sunday 2nd

We left the wharf at Cooktown at 7 AM. & are now once more on our way. It is a beautiful day, the sea as calm as glass.

Monday 3rd

Anchored a mile or 2 from Townsville at 12 o'clock today. A pilot came on board shortly after tiffin & took us on a little distance to the coal hulk, where we remain until tomorrow. It is too far to go ashore.

Tuesday 4th

We left Townsville at noon with a fair wind & calm sea. We shall probably arrive in Brisbane on Saturday.

Wednesday 5th

Windy & cold all day. The first cold weather for months. It was a little rough this morning coming through "Whitsunday" Pass but only while we were coming through, it has been calm ever since.

---

97 Tiffin – of Indian origin, a light meal, especially of curried dishes and fruit, lunch.

Appendix

Poems

Why are we Troubled?

Are we right to be desponding on our way,
And to chafe against the worries of each day?
To rebel, with restless spirit at our lot –
Is this right, if we are Christians?
Surely not!

If we only just could simply understand
That our life is safe with Jesus in His hand,
And would tell to Him in secret every care,
And would take to Him each trouble hard to bear;

And when pressed with sore temptation, would depend
Upon Him, our tried and ever faithful Friend, –
Then the peace He left His people long ago
Would be ours, in storm or sunshine weal or woe.

Calm as that moonbeam on the wall,
Sleep broods[1] on baby's eyes.
Arms, hushed and still, but pulsing quick
Enfold him as he lies;
My brain is full of thronging thoughts,
Strange passions thrill my breast,
My heart aches with a load of love
That will not let me rest.

Lord, let him shelter in my arms,
Or take us both to Thine;
Or if a troublous life must come,
Make all the trouble mine.
Or let Thy sharp words pierce my heart
To blunt them for the child –
What care I, Lord, for stain and shame
So he keep undefiled!

The dim years stand about my bed
They neither smile nor weep,
Like softest kisses on my face
The little fingers creep.
I hear slow footfalls, in the night,
Of fate upon his track.
O, love I cannot let you go!
I cannot keep you back!

Nay, Lord I know not what I ask
I know not how to pray.
Hear Thou the crying Mother-soul,
And not the words I say.
Do Thou what seemeth good to Thee
So he be spared from sin;
And oh! If love can aught avail,
Let mine be counted in.

---

1 broods – covers, as with wings.

The Diary of Emily Caroline Creaghe, Explorer

Recipes

Sea Pie

Line a good sized bowl with paste made with fresh beef suet.
Cut into small pieces 1 lb of beef. Lay it on the bottom of the bowl; slice 1 onion, sprinkle a handful of flour over. Add a little pepper & salt. Cover all this over with water. Then fill up the bowl with potatoes that have been peeled and lying in cold water a little while, cover the bowl with a lid of the paste, tie a clean cloth tightly round & plunge into boiling water. Boil for 2 hours quickly.

Damper

To 1 lb of flour 1/2 a teaspoonful of soda, & 1/2 of acid, or 1 teaspoonful of baking powder, Enough milk or water to mix this into a stiff dough. Knead well.

Puffs

Beat very light the yolks of 6 eggs 1 pint of milk, a pinch of salt: the whites of the eggs beaten to a froth & flour enough to make the batter like a thick cream. Bake in cups in quick oven.

Carl Creek Recipes

Tea-Cake

Into a quart of flour, 1 teaspoonful carbonate of soda, 2 teaspoonfuls cream of Tartar (or 1 of acid) & a good pinch of salt, 1 tablespoon of butter (or dripping) & add enough milk to give it the consistency of a stiff batter. Drop pieces into a greased tin, a short distance apart, & bake immediately in a quick over for 15 minutes – To be eaten hot or cold.

Numinum Cake

3 eggs, 1 cup of sugar, 1 cup flour, 1 third teaspoon soda, 1 teaspoon cream tartar, lemon peel. Beat eggs well & stir all together quickly & bake in a quick oven. The batter 3/4 of an inch thick.

Plain Cake

1 lb flour 1/4 lb sugar, 1/4 lb currants 1/4 lb sultanas, a little candied peel, 1 teaspoon ginger, 1 teaspoon carbonate soda. Mix well with a large cupful of butter milk. Bake about an hour & a half.

Snow Eggs

A custard of 4 eggs & cup 1/2 of milk the whites used by beating to thick froth and putting on the fire – no lumps – in boiling water for a minute, turning them once.

Auntie's cakes.

Ingredients – 1 lb Maizena, 2 teaspoons Baking powder. Rind of 3 small lemons – 1/2 lb sifted sugar – 3/4 lb butter – 4 eggs
Cut lemon peel to shreds & chop finely, mix the dry ingredients into a stiff batter with the eggs well beaten. Put a teaspoonful into each little patty-tin & bake 5 minutes in rather a quick oven –

Guava Jelly

Take 10 lbs guavas of which the greatest part must be green & not one guava over ripe. Over ripe fruit spoils both the flavor & consistency of jelly. Cut the guavas in half & put them into the preserving pan with water over 2 qrts water. Let them simmer gently over a moderate fire till the fruit is all quite tender. Strain through a coarse linen cloth, squeezing till dry. – To each qrt of juice add twice the quantity of sugar. Scald the pan & replace the sweetened juice. Stir gently over the fire – till sugar is dissolved. Remove the scum as it forms. In from 30 to 40 min, the liquid should have become a dark color. Drop a little of the jelly into a saucer of cold water. If it congeals it is ready, if not go on boiling very gently till it does. Strain through muslin or flannel cloth.

To utilise the skins & seeds
Add 1 lb sugar to each lb of the seeds & skins left in the straining cloth. Place in pan with very little water if the sweetened fruit is quite dry. Stir over slow fire till quite thick 30 or 40 min.

Letter to Her Father

Part of a letter written by Emily Caroline Creaghe to her father (Major George Cayley Robinson in Sydney)

Telegraph Station "Katherine"
260 miles south of Port Darwin

July 12th 1883

My dearest Papa

We have arrived safely so far at last, and hope to get to the end of our journey (Port Darwin) in a few weeks' time. I suppose you received Harry's telegram from Powell's Creek in May, telling you of our safe arrival there. Our horses were so knocked up at that stage, having had such hard work, and several long stages without water, that Harry and I were obliged to come on here with five of the worst horses, and Mr. Favenc went out with 9 others to finish the exploring on the McArthur River. We will give you full particulars of our trip when we see you, as the account is much too long and interesting to write about. You will be glad to hear that I was not in the slightest degree unwell the whole way. Poor Harry was very ill with dysentery for 10 days during the trip, at which time I was very anxious. We had one encounter with wild blacks, but there was no harm done. Sufficient of the trip until I see you – Your letters forwarded from Normanton to Port Darwin we got this afternoon from Hongkong! where they were carried on in mistake. There is a weekly mail from Port Darwin to this station, so we hope to get more news by the next Southern Mail. The latest we have of any of you is the middle of April. We are so sorry to hear the sad news about the mines, and at Louie's absence.[1] I do hope she is with you again, it is miserable to think of your being alone. Poor Jim, too. I cannot imagine how he managed to get into such trouble – when we shall be down I don't quite know. We are waiting for Favenc

---

1 Creaghe's father had invested in gold mines in Gympie. Severe floods there meant that he incurred heavy losses, which might in turn help to explain the absence of Louie, Creaghe's stepmother.

to come in, and to settle up money matters. Harry is getting rather anxious about him as he is a fortnight over the time he expected to be out. If he is not in by the end of this month Harry will be obliged to organise a search party, and go out after him. In that case, I may go down without Harry, he following when either Favenc or his remains are found. The Blacks are very dangerous on the McArthur, so we have need to be anxious on his account. When I was staying in the Gulf, I sold my silver watch for £4, which I send to you, it being yours by rights, you having given me my beautiful gold one. I would not have sold it, but that I was offfered so much more than you gave for it, and you were not so well off as you used to be. I never used it in town, so the £4 is of much more service to you than the watch was to me. If Favenc turns up safely before the end of the month, we shall be with you in the end of August. Harry would very much like [. . .]

Portrait of Caroline Creaghe as an older woman at Circular Quay
Smith Family

AFTERWORD

After the expedition Harry and Caroline returned to Sydney for the birth of their child, conceived during the expedition. In 1882 they had tragically lost their first son, Cayley. Gerald Harry Percy Creaghe came into the world on 19 January 1884. He accompanied his parents on their return to Queensland, where Harry found work, initally on a dairy farm and later on Apis Creek cattle station outside Rockhampton. It seems that his work took him back to the Northern Territory, at least for a period, and in all probability unaccompanied by his family. Evidence places him at Hodgson Downs station in late 1884 and the first half of 1885, almost certainly as manager and possibly even as a part-owner.[1]

Alas, Gerald was just 2 years old when his father was taken from him in tragic circumstances. The explorer David Lindsay, who had met the Creaghes during their expedition in the Northern Territory, many years later reported the death as follows: "While breaking in a young mare he was wearing a ring, an heirloom, about which there was attached a tradition that he who lost it would meet with a violent death. In a struggle with the mare, Creaghe who had become thin through fever, lost the ring. He then related the prophecy, saying 'I expect that mare will be the death of me.' Next day she dashed into a tree and Creaghe was killed."[2]

Harry at that time – 6 August 1886 – was just 37 years of age; he was buried in Rockhampton cemetery. A few months later, on Boxing Day of that year, his third child, Harry Percy Archer-Butler Creaghe, was born.

Of all the expeditioners, Lindsay Crawford was the one with the most enduring links with the Northern Territory. Before the

---

1   The evidence comes from the *Northern Territory Gazette* on 17.5.1884 and, on several occasions, from the *Northern Territory Times*. I am indebted to Tony Roberts for this information.
2   From the 26 August 1920 edition of an unnamed publication, in "Excerpts from Newspapers" deposited in Emily Caroline Creaghe collection, Mitchell Library, ML MSS 2982. Lindsay has Creaghe dying at Hodgson Downs in the Northern Territory, though this might be apocryphal.

expedition he had already become a kind of Territorian by choice; after it he gained employment at Richmond Downs station and then at Victoria River Downs, where he was appointed full-time manager in 1884. Alas, in the time he was there conditions did not grow any easier; he had to contend with endemic malaria, logistical nightmares and chronically antagonistic relations with the indigenous population. Under the most trying of conditions he earned the respect of his men, who on the eve of his departure in 1890 praised him as "always considerate and obliging to those around you."[3] Crawford returned to his default career of telegrapher in 1897, though without abandoning his adopted homeland. From 1900 he headed a line party, only to die within a year at the age of just 48. Officially the cause of death was dysentery, though another interpretation has it that hunger, wet (he had been unable to light a fire) and deteriorating mental faculties (papers of the time claimed that he was sensible "up to within a short time of his death") played a role.[4] The place of his demise was Sturt's Plain, just north of Newcastle Waters, where the ground there was so hard that a colleague, W. Holtze, needed a tomahawk to dig his grave.[5]

Favenc proved more durable, though not by much. Even well before the 1883 expedition he had shown himself to be multi-talented, complementing his activities as a bushman and explorer with a love of writing. He made a name for himself as a prolific writers of stories, novels and verse published in a variety of places, including the *Queenslander*, the *Sydney Mail* and the *Bulletin*. After the expedition with the Creaghes he even turned his gifted hand to history, writing a very thorough account of one hundred years of Australian exploration.[6] In it his own name – though not that of Caroline

---

3   Cited in J. Makin, "Lindsay Crawford", in *Northern Territory Dictionary of Biography. Vol. One: To 1945*, ed. David Carment, Robyn Maynard, Alan Powell, Darwin: NTU Press, 1990, p. 68
4   Makin, p. 68.
5   Makin, p. 68.
6   Ernest Favenc, *The History of Australian Exploration from 1788 to 1888. Compiled from State Documents, Private Papers and the Most Authentic Sources of Information*, Sydney: Turner and Henderson, 1888.

Creaghe nor of any other member of the 1883 expdition – appeared comfortably beside those of such luminaries as Charles Sturt, Edward John Eyre, Robert O'Hara Burke, William John Wills, Ernest Giles and John Forrest.

It was some time before Favenc turned his hand to exploration again. The year was 1888, and Favenc's interest remained in the far outback, but on this occasion it was the outback of Western Australia. Beginning in Geraldton in March, and with backing from an English syndicate, he spent some months in the territory of the upper Gascoyne and the Ashburton Rivers. In the following year a report on the expedition was published in the *Proceedings of the Royal Geographical Society*.[7]

Thereafter Favenc turned his hand increasingly to his literary talents to support himself and his family. He was a prolific writer of short stories, but he also produced a number of books and novels.[8] So central was his literary activity to the latter part of his life that he has been described as "the Lawson of the Far Outback."[9] Premature poor health meant that his exploring days were over, though he did manage a journey to New Guinea and parts of the Pacific in 1901. His last great work was on a topic which remained close to his heart – *The Explorers of Australia and Their Life Work*. It was published in 1908, the year of Favenc's death in Sydney at the age of 62. An obituary in the *Bulletin*, which over the years had published so much of Favenc's work, underlined the dramatic and premature decline in his health over the preceding years: "The figure of a tall thin stooping man, drawn face, and short grey beard, making its way with the help of a stick, and strangely feeble steps down Kellett-street and William-street to the Park and city of a morning will have been noticed by

---

7   Ernest Favenc, "Explorations in the Region of the Upper Gascoyne and Ashburton Rivers, West Australia", *Proceedings of the Royal Geographical Society* IX (1989), pp. 490–95.
8   The most comprehensive listing of his literary output is in Cheryl Taylor (ed.), *Ernest Favenc. Tales of the Austral Tropics*, Sydney: UNSW Press, 1997, 163–82. This publication also contains a number of Favenc's short stories.
9   Annie McCormick, Derek McDonnell and Jonathan Wantrup, *Frontiers: Experience on the Australian Frontiers 1788–1950*, Sydney: Hordern House: 1991, p. 288.

many. But those who come that way to town will miss that figure now."[10]

* * *

By far the most enduring of the members of the 1883 expedition was Caroline Creaghe. When Harry died in 1886 she had one young child to care for and was pregnant with the next. For a time she ran a guest-house in Rockhampton before being engaged as a housekeeper at Tooloombah station. She met Joseph Jupp Smallman Barnett, an Englishman born in 1849, who, as a station manager near Rockhampton, had known Harry. Indeed, Joseph had promised Harry that he would look after Caroline in the case of Harry's early death. By his first marriage Joseph had already had three children, though the first two girls had drowned at the ages of just two and five. The third and surviving child was Lumley George, born 30 March 1883, while Caroline was exploring. A fourth child followed, but Joseph divorced his wife, claiming that the child was not his own.

Caroline and Joseph married in December 1889, so that she now became Emily Caroline Barnett. She brought with her to the family her two children, the five-year-old Gerald and the four-year-old Harry Pierce; Joseph brought with him Lumley, by then aged six. In a short time the family grew further. Twins – Eric John and Lionel Tom – were born in November 1890. Lilla Mavis followed in 1893, Jessie Moira in 1896, Harold Douglas in 1899 and Evelyn Roy in 1902. Thus altogether Caroline bore nine children and brought up eight of them, as well as Lumley, their half-brother.

The strains of caring for a large family in the harsh conditions of a cattle station in rural Queensland did not, however, mean that her life was without incident or adventure. Ten years into her second marriage she undertook a voyage to New Zealand aboard the *Perthshire* with five of her children, one of them just nine months old. Almost catastrophic mechanical failure meant that the vessel floated uncontrollably through the Tasman Sea for some seven weeks before rescue. Nor was her life devoid of further tragedy. In

---

10 Bulletin, 16 November 1908, p. 18.

1917 Harry Pierce killed someone by the name of Mr Morton in a shooting accident. Caroline wrote in a letter, "If Harry had remembered my teaching of not shooting on Sunday, this terrible accident would never have happened. I expect he wishes now that he had kept to the old Sunday ways, indeed he will wish it to his dying day poor dear boy."[11] Lionel Tom Barnett enlisted in the AIF and was killed in France in 1918. In October of 1922, and after a long struggle with cancer which, in the final years, demanded Caroline's constant care, her husband Joseph Barnett died. Caroline's oldest surviving child, Harry Creaghe, having bought a sugar cane farm near Cairns, fell from a bridge and incurred serious brain damage. He died in 1930 leaving three sons, all of whom joined the AIF in the Second World War. All of them suffered greatly in their campaigns in North Africa, and two of them died young.

After the second marriage Caroline lived for some twenty years on Marlborough station, which her husband managed, and then for some 12 years settled in Rockhampton, where she ran a guest-house. Of this period in her life, her youngest son Evelyn Roy Barnett later wrote, "She still kept up her 'standards', dressing for dinner every night. She put on her own church services every Sunday night for the family. When in Rockhampton nothing pleased her more than to file into St. Pauls Catherdral with several of her children and any others that she was able to collect."[12] Eventually she returned with her husband to Sydney, where she lived in Roseville – where Joseph died – and then in Mosman. A photograph captures her quite late in her life at Circular Quay. She enjoyed excellent health for most of her life, and indeed reported to her youngest son that "the only headache she had ever had was when her second daughter was born!" In the Second World War, as in the First, she actively performed volunteer work, knitting, spinning and helping in the Red Cross tea room. But during a spell in a convalescent home after a bout of back trouble and sciatica she slipped on a polished floor and broke a hip. Thereafter her health was irreversibly compromised; she died on Armistice Day 1944 at the age of 84.

---

11   Letter by Emily Caroline Creaghe, Smith family archive.
12   Recollections of E. Roy Barnett, Smith family archive.

INDEX

A

Augustus Downs Station   23

B

Baines, Mr. (of E & A Bank)   95–97
Barnett Family (from Caroline's second marriage)   vii, 110, 111
Bowen   8, 15–17
Bowley, Mr. (at Powell's Creek)   61–66
Burns Philp & Co.   19, 20

C

Carl Creek Station (the Shadforths' Lilydale Station)   vii, 9, 10, 24–39, 102–104
Channel Island Lightship   17
Chester, Capt. & Mrs. (at Thursday Island)   15–18, 20, 99
Clark, Mr (Native Police)   37–38
Cooktown   9, 17, 98, 99
Corea (vessel, Sydney to Thursday Island)   15–18, 20, 99
Crawford, Lindsay (member of exploration party)   8–12, 39–66, 77, 82, 86, 88, 89, 106–108
Crawford, Mr. (pastoralist killed)   13, 37, 38
Creaghe Family   viii, 2, 107, 110, 111
Cuthbertson, Mr. (with David Lindsay)   85–87

D

Daly Waters Telegraph Station   12, 66–68, 70–73, 77, 82
Darwin. *See* Port Darwin *and* Palmerston
Davies, Eliza   8
Doyle, Mr.   25, 28, 31, 34, 35, 38

E

Elsey Telegraph Station   72–74, 86

F

Favenc, Bessie   vii, 6–9, 18, 19, 20, 95, 96
Favenc, Ernest   2–20, 11 (illust.), 39–66, 77, 82, 85, 86, 88, 95, 96, 105, 106, 108–110
Feilung (vessel, Thursday Island to Normanton)   12, 96–99
Flinders, Matthew   3
Flinders Telegraph Station   19
Foelsche, Paul Heinrich Matthias   87, 88, 93–95, 95 (illust.), 97
Forsyth, Mr. (manager Burns Philp)   19

G

Giles, Mr. (Alfred) and Mrs. (of Springvale Station)   11, 12, 75, 77–83, 86–97
Goss, Mr. (assistant, Powell's Creek)   61–72
Gregory, Augustus   3, 12 (illust.)

H

Hann, Frank 26 (illust.)   27, 31, 32
Hodgson Downs   107
Hope, Capt. (Albinia Downs)   1, 2
Hughes Mr. C.W. (Springvale)   77–79, 81–84

J

Janson, Mr. (goldmine owner, Pine Creek)   91
Johns, Mr. (station master, Daly Waters)   70–72, 76, 82, 84, 88, 89
Johnson, Mr. and Mrs. (Southport Telegraph Station)   93, 94

K

Katherine (Telegraph Station)   vii, 11, 63, 65, 71, 72, 74–77, 80–90, 93
Kemp, Mr. (assistant, Daly Waters Station)   70–76

L

Lamb, Dr. William   1, 2, 31, 38
Lamond, Mr. (Inspector of Native Police)   24, 25, 27, 28, 30–32, 34, 38
Leichhardt, Ludwig   3, 6 (illust.), 12 (illust.), 21, 24

Lilydale Station *(see also* Carl Creek Station*)*   viii, 9, 24–39
Lindsay, David   85–87, 86 (illust.), 107
Lizard Island   17
Lorne Hill Station   26, 27, 31
Lukin, Gresley   4, 5

M
McKinlay, John   4
McMinn, Gilbert Rotherdale   83, 84, 94–97
Magowrah Station   20
Margaret Vale Station   31, 33
Morstone Station   26
Murray, Mr. (Morstone Station)   20–23, 26, 33, 38
Murray, Mr. and Mrs. (Katherine Telegraph Station)   viii, 63, 75–90

N
Native Police   25, 28, 37
Normanton   2, 9, 19–21, 23, 25, 72, 105

P
Palmerston (Port Darwin)   5, 14, 65, 88–90, 93, 94–97, 100 (illust.)
Pine Creek (Janson's gold mine)   91
Powell's Creek   8, 10–12, 58, 60–66, 72, 77, 105
Port Darwin   2, 4, 5, 8–10, 12, 38, 61, 63, 65, 75, 82, 88, 93, 94, 97, 105
Port Douglas   16, 17
Price, Edward W.   84

R
Robinson, Charles James (Charlie, Caroline's brother)   18
Robinson, Harriet (Lilla, Caroline's sister)   1, 2, 31, 38
Robinson, Jessie (Caroline's sister)   27
Robinson, Maj. George Cayley, (Papa, Caroline's father)   viii, 1, 15, 27, 31, 38, 63, 79, 83, 84, 99, 105, 106
Robinson, Mary Harriet (Mamma, Caroline's mother)   1, 33
Robinson, Mary (Minnie, Caroline's sister)   31, 38, 85

S
Shackle Telegraph Station (Yam Creek)   92
Shadforth, Mr. Francis & Family, (Lilydale Station, Carl Creek)
    viii, 20, 21, 24–39
Solomon, Alice & Vaiben Louis   95–97
Southport   8, 89 (illust.), 93, 96 (illust.)
Springvale Station   11, 75, 77–90, 85 (illust.)
Stuart, John McDouall   3, 4, 12 (illust.), 71
Sturt, Charles   8

T
Thursday Island   9, 17–19, 25 (illust.), 28, 98
Todd, Charles & Mt. Todd   90
Townsville   8, 16, 19, 99
Truganini (vessel, Thursday Island to Normanton)   9, 19, 20
Tucker, Captain   18
Tuckfield, Mr. (The Elsey station master)   73, 74

W
Warner (Mr. Murray's man)   9, 22, 23
Watson Bros., & family (Gregory Downs Station)   24, 39
Watson, Mary (Lizard Island)   17
Watson, Mr. (Harry's friend from Augustus Downs Station)
    22–24
Watson, Mr. Jack   26, 27, 31, 32
Willis, Mr. (Margaret Vale Station)   31, 33–35

Y
Yam Creek (The Shackle)   92

Wakefield Press is an independent publishing and
distribution company based in Adelaide, South Australia.
We love good stories and publish beautiful books.
To see our full range of books, please visit our website at
www.wakefieldpress.com.au
where all titles are available for purchase.
To keep up with our latest releases, news and events,
subscribe to our monthly newsletter.

Find us!

Facebook: www.facebook.com/wakefield.press
Twitter: www.twitter.com/wakefieldpress
Instagram: www.instagram.com/wakefieldpress

www.ingramcontent.com/pod-product-compliance
Lightning Source LLC
Chambersburg PA
CBHW020418230426
43663CB00007BA/1216